**W9-AMZ-858**

# WRITERS REVEALED

Rosemary Hartill was born in Shropshire and read English at Bristol University. After working in publishing for six years, she became a freelance broadcaster for the BBC. In 1979, she was appointed Religious Affairs Reporter, and in 1982, in succession to Gerald Priestland, Religious Affairs Correspondent – only the second woman correspondent ever to be appointed to BBC Radio, UK. She has contributed regularly to the BBC's news services, including the World Service, and was nominated for the 'Reporter of the Year' in the 1987 Sony Radio Awards. She has also worked on a number of TV magazine and documentary programmes.

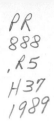

# WRITERS
# REVEALED

— • —

## ROSEMARY HARTILL

## PETER BEDRICK BOOKS
### NEW YORK

For my parents, with love

First American edition published in 1989 by
Peter Bedrick Books, New York
by agreement with BBC Books, London

Library of Congress Cataloging-in-Publication Data
Hartill, Rosemary.
Writers revealed: faith, religion, and God in the life and work of
eight contemporary novelists./Rosemary Hartill.
p. ca.
"First American edition"—T.p. verso.
ISBN 0-87226-329-0.—ISBN 0-87226-220-0 (pbk.)
1. English fiction—20th century—History and criticism. 2. Novelists, English—20th century—Religious life. 3. Religion and literature—History—20th century. 4. Novelists, English—20th century—Interviews. 5. Faith in literature. 6. God in literature.
I. Title.
PR888.R5H37   1989
823'.91409—dc20                                              89-33259
                                                                CIP

Manufactured in the United States of America

∞

The paper used in this book complies with the Permanent
Paper Standard issued by the National Information Standards Organization (Z39.48-1984).

10 9 8 7 6 5 4 3 2 1

# CONTENTS

— • —

'Many suffer from the incurable disease of writing, and it becomes chronic in their sick minds.'

JUVENAL AD c.60 – c.130


'If a man write a better book, preach a better sermon, or make a better mouse trap than his neighbour, tho' he build his house in the woods, the world will make a beaten path to his door.'

EMERSON

# INTRODUCTION

— • —

Why do so many men and women suffer from what Juvenal called 'the incurable disease' of writing? How do their personal beliefs influence the way they write and the subjects they choose? And how does the creative process work? It was to explore questions like these, that in June and July 1989, BBC Radio broadcast a series of interviews with eight of the foremost British novelists writing today. The purpose was to ask a number of well-known authors to talk in some depth about their work and their life. The aim was to try and throw more light on some of the things that mattered most deeply to them. This book, *Writers Revealed*, is based on that series.

Although I had originally begun working for the BBC as a general broadcaster, for several years I had reported about belief in Britain and around the world as the BBC's religious affairs correspondent. I now wanted to move quite away from the usual 'religious' voices of Christianity and other faiths, and to talk to other people about their lives and outlook, about what beliefs and ideas absorb them. My degree had been in English literature, and for six years after leaving university I had worked in publishing. So the world of books and of fiction seemed a natural place to return to.

But which novelists should David Coomes, the producer, invite to create the series?

Various names immediately bubbled up. Some we were unable to include. Graham Greene, for example, and William Golding hardly ever give interviews, and refused. Muriel Spark said yes, but it was not possible, sadly, to pin her down, for this series anyway, to a place, a date and a time.

One thing struck us specially as a list was drawn up: the predominance of Catholics or lapsed Catholics (Anthony Burgess, Brian Moore, Piers Paul Read, Muriel Spark, Graham Greene). Catholicism, as it was taught fifty years or so ago, entered people's bloodstream. For some, it became the lifeblood itself; for others, it was a virus that had to be thrown off, a threat to health and vitality, to light and life. But neither the acceptance nor the rejection was ever that simple. Illuminating light would pierce what seemed like shrouding darkness; people who had never been inside a church for twenty-five years would feel suddenly drawn to recommit themselves to God; others would feel hopeless and leave. Catholicism exercises power over people's most intimate lives, sometimes brutally. It embraces centuries and continents. It tells stories about saints and martyrs, noble and ignoble people. It makes Catholics strangers in this world, because it speaks of their true everlasting home being elsewhere. And it displays its teachings in glowing metaphors, symbols and images. No wonder that so many novelists come from that tradition, both loving and loathing it, both rejecting and accepting it, both living out of it and dying in it.

By contrast, none of the names on the list came from the Free Church tradition. Indeed some branches of Presbyterianism are marked by the literalness which which they have interpreted, and therefore often misinterpreted, Catholic metaphorical language. Once, the Free Churches produced great imaginative writers like Bunyan. Even today, week in, week out, Methodist congregations are still offered sweeping poetic images of faith in the hymns of Charles Wesley. But when John and Charles Wesley died, Methodism gradually lost its fire, its energy. It got bogged down in committees, writing minutes, its glowing coals doused with non-alcoholic wine, followed by hymn sandwiches.

Some of that energy and sheer goodness still survives. But goodness has not necessarily much to do with novel-writing, even if energy has. And some of those people may agree with those moments of Brian Moore's life when he questions his profession. Wouldn't it be better, they wonder, helping the dispossessed, say, in India, or, rather more immediately, Mrs Carter down the street? This view disregards the titanic effort of great art to provide a vision, to reveal how things are, what truly matters.

None of the authors in conversation in this book are in the

mass-market league; some of them are read much more widely than others, but they all produce well-reviewed novels with a consistently intellectual core; and they are all, at one level or another, interested in how and what to believe, of how to interpret the world in ways that can be understood in language that speaks both to the mind and the heart.

With each writer, I found myself exploring a different area of experience. Anthony Burgess, perhaps the most international of Britain's composers, linguists and literary figures, recalled the coarser side of Catholic culture into which he was introduced as a child in working-class Manchester. Still claiming to be a believer, he is not at all pleased, however, with the Catholic Church's efforts since the Second Vatican Council in the 1960s to draw him and others back as practising Catholics.

Then there is Bernice Rubens, in whose bizarre, wonderful and – literally – fantastic novels the grotesque failures and inadequacies of the human heart are just about (sometimes) saved by love (or pity, or gentleness, or kindness). Lately, she has been fighting off with mocking humour the persistent, demanding, Jewish God who undermines her atheist preferences.

John Mortimer describes why to him a celestial judge would be even worse than the human variety he knows and loathes. He finds God 'an incredible bastard', and was puzzled that bishops with whom he had raised the question gave such unsatisfactory answers and had not, apparently, been thinking about it for a long time. When I suggested that the god he described was not, in fact, very like the god most Christians believed in, he responded that Christianity was whatever you wanted it to be . . .

Iris Murdoch describes how, to her, Plato is king, and how he established the notion that human life is about the battle of good and evil. Though attracted to Buddhism, she explains why she regards herself as a Christian even though she does not believe in the Resurrection or the divinity of Christ, nor the afterlife. She is now the author of twenty-three novels, each new book planned out in intricate detail before she puts a word on paper.

A. N. Wilson, too, was absorbed not with the doctrines and structures of belief, but with the figure of Jesus, and with the sadly failed efforts of that great genius Tolstoy, whose biography he published last year, to live out the ideals of the Sermon on the Mount. Technically, he is increasingly interested in the problem of realism – how far the novelist distorts truth by patterning it apparently realistically, but in fact artificially, into narrative. That problem absorbed earlier artists like James Joyce and Virginia Woolf for years.

Sara Maitland delights in risks, experimenting with different forms. In an East End vicarage, she dreams of woman friends two thousand years old and more, met in the pages of the Old and New Testaments. Her use of biblical stories to parallel feminist and socialist attitudes today seems sometimes to do violence to the context, but I was struck by the excitement and clarity of her experience of the abundance and generosity of the Creator.

To Brian Moore, faith is a gift he does not have, though he says he envies those who do. In his story-telling, he often portrays belief and the loss or testing of it, with the detached skill of a surgeon (his father's profession), and to establish the right mood at the start of a novel, he may rewrite the opening pages forty or fifty times. But the modest interview he gave does not capture the sheer compassion with which he writes in, for example, *The Lonely Passion of Judith Hearne*.

Finally Piers Paul Read, who writes with the hope that he can influence the lives of his readers to a more catholic view of reality. Conscious that his own beliefs (which include the conviction that there is a personal devil in each of us, sowing seeds of dissatisfaction and dangerous illusion) are alien to many of his contemporary writers, the sense of being an outsider is central to his writing.

In fact, that sense of being an outsider, for one reason or another, is common to all the novelists in this book. Sometimes the exile was self-imposed (Brian Moore escaping to America from Ireland), sometimes it is linked with racial history (Bernice Rubens), sometimes it is rooted in the earliest personal childhood memories (John Mortimer, the son of a blind father). One effect is the shared need to try and describe how things are, to understand what they might mean and what, in the end, lasts best. I hope this book will help to reveal and share with others at least *part* of the journey taken by these eight novelists.

Rosemary Hartill
February 1989

# ANTHONY BURGESS

— • —

BA; Hon. DLitt; born 25 February, 1917; married 1942, Llewela
Isherwood Jones, BA (d. 1968); married 1968, Liliana
Macellari; one son. Education: Xaverian College, Manchester;
Manchester University Served Army, 1940–6. Lecturer:
Birmingham University Extra-Mural Dept, 1946–8; Ministry of
Education, 1948–50; English Master, Banbury Grammar
School, 1950–4; Education Officer, Malaya and Brunei,
1954–9. Visiting Fellow, Princeton University, 1970–1.
Distinguished Professor, City College, New York, 1972–3. Hon.
DLitt, Manchester, 1982. Commandeur: de Mérite Culturel,
Monaco; des Arts and des Lettres, France. **TV scripts**: *Moses the
Lawgiver and Jesus of Nazareth* (series), 1977. **Radio**: *Blooms of
Dublin*, 1982 (musical). **Publications**: *Time for a Tiger*, 1956;
*The Enemy in a Blanket*, 1958; *Beds in the East*, 1959 (these
three, as *The Malayan Trilogy*, 1972, and as *The Long Day
Wanes*, 1982); *The Right to an Answer*, 1960; *The Doctor is
Sick*, 1960; *The Worm and the Ring*, 1961; *Devil of a State*,
1951; *A Clockwork Orange*, 1962 (filmed 1971); *The Wanting
Seed*, 1962; *Honey for the Bears*, 1963; *The Novel Today*,
1963; *Language Made Plain*, 1964; *Nothing Like the Sun*, 1964;
*The Eve of St Venus*, 1964; *A Vision of Battlements*, 1965; *Here
Comes Everybody – an Introduction to James Joyce*, 1965;
*Tremor of Intent*, 1966; *A Shorter Finnegan's Wake*, 1966; *The
Novel Now*, 1967; *Enderby Outside*, 1968; *Urgent Copy*, 1968;
*Shakespeare*, 1970; *MF*, 1976; *A Long Trip to Teatime*, 1976;
*Beard's Roman Women*, 1976; *ABBA, ABBA*, 1977; *New
York*, 1977; *L'Homme de Nazareth*, 1977 (*Man of Nazareth*,
1979); *Ernest Hemingway and His World*, 1978; 1985, 1978;
*They Wrote in English* (Italy, 1979); *The Land Where the Ice-
Cream Grows*, 1979; *Earthly Powers*, 1980; *On Going to Bed*,
1982; *This Man and Music*, 1982; *The End of the World News*,

1982; *Enderby's Dark Lady*, 1984; *Ninety-Nine Novels*, 1984; *The Kingdom of the Wicked*, 1985; *Flame into Being*, 1985; *The Pianoplayers*, 1986; (trans, Rostand) *Cyrano de Bergerac*, 1971; (trans, Sophocles) *Oedipus the King*, 1973. **Translations of stage plays**: *Homage to Qwer Yuiop*, 1986; as Joseph Kell: *One Hand Clapping*, 1961; *Inside Mr Enderby*, 1963; as John Burgess Wilson: *English Literature: A Survey for Students*, 1958. Contributor to the *Observer*, the *Spectator*, the *Listener*, *Encounter, Queen, Times Literary Supplement, Hudson Review, Holiday, Playboy, American Scholar, Corriere della Sera, Le Monde*, etc. **Autobiography**: *Little Wilson and Big God*, 1987.

# UNEARTHLY POWERS

— • —

'Oh, I've never been an atheist,' said Anthony Burgess, with vigour. 'I don't think I have ever touched that particular abyss. I think it is possible for Graham Greene and other pseudo-Catholic writers to doubt the existence of God. I have never been able to doubt the existence of God. . . . But whether really this affects the way I live, I don't know.'

We were talking down a radio line. I was in a studio in Newcastle, hemmed in by a glass window and three panels of switches. He was in London. The briefness of this most international of Britain's composers, linguists and literary figures' visit to Britain from his home in Monaco had made communications problematic. So, I had no option but to imagine his narrowed blue eyes, darting sharp nervous glances from right to left, the long sweep of thinning hair combed round his head, the gestures as he puffed his usual slim Panatellas.

We had been discussing whether a good novelist could ever be a holy person. The main character of his epic 650-page novel *Earthly Powers*, himself a successful novelist, had certainly doubted it. Kenneth Toomey is first introduced on page one, line one, on the afternoon of his eighty-first birthday, in bed with his thirty-five-year-old catamite. To write novels, Toomey believes, a writer has to touch pitch and be defiled.

Mr Burgess couldn't remember putting those words into Mr Toomey's mouth, but yes, he did think that to take up the trade of a novelist was to some extent to forfeit the right to sainthood. He could imagine a poet like Gerard Manley Hopkins being

canonised, or possibly, John Donne. But the nature of the
novelist's craft, on the other hand, is to look at life as it is lived – a
life more full of sin and squalor than sanctity.

To suggest that a saint couldn't quite look at life as it was lived
struck me as a disappointing idea of a saint. But that seems to be
how Anthony Burgess believes the Vatican regards saints. If he
himself were put in charge of canonisations in a dark, whispering
office somewhere in the Vatican, a new wind would soon be
whirling the dusty piles of depositions. For a start, a few animals
might be canonised. He had often felt when he was living or
travelling in North Africa that there had to be a heaven to accommodate the donkeys that bore such heavy burdens without
murmur.

As for humans, 'No', I could imagine him declaring, deleting
with gusto in heavy blue pencil the proposed name of some
etiolated piety. 'Not sufficiently Rabelaisian.' But he had, he said,
met one or two people he regarded as saints. One was his cousin,
the former Roman Catholic Archbishop of Birmingham, George
Patrick Dwyer. Archbishop Dwyer's death in 1987 deprived the
Catholic bishops of England and Wales of one of their few splashes
of old-fashioned colour.

'He wasn't ascetic; he kept a good table; he grew fat. But he had
a quality of total realism, he accepted evil and good not as mere
philosophical propositions, but as real, solid things. He did his
doctoral thesis on Charles Baudelaire, and he knew all about sin,
all about evil. But his capacity to remain optimistic and believe
that good would finally prevail made him somewhat saintly.'

We agreed that it is unlikely George Patrick Dwyer will ever be
canonised.

Anthony Burgess's belief in God, together with his affection for
the Rabelasisian and his detestation of Jane Austen, grew out of his
Catholic upbringing in the 1920s in a working-class area of Manchester. His father was a pianist in cinemas and music halls, whose
second wife, a pub landlady, seems to have doled out affection for
her stepson only in economical packages. He was brought up in the
atmosphere of a slightly slummy public house and later of a more
respectable off-licence. He says now he was then too young really
to appreciate it.

'People were wallowing in drink most of the time, fighting each other, singing, and the rest of it. It was life. It was the warm fug of life.'

One lasting effect, he says, is that the coarse, the rough, became part of his make-up. 'This makes certain lady critics dislike me as a writer.' He did not seem to regard this as a great tragedy.

To Burgess, the coarse and the rough are just one aspect of Catholic culture. He feels that the kind of life he has lived has been totally conditioned by the Catholicism in which he grew up. 'When Rabelais wrote his great book *Gargantua and Pantagruel*, he was not really glorifying vomit and defecation and drunkenness, he was telling a symbolic story in which we are all thirsty for the faith, and the wine or beer or drunkenness is a kind of symbol of religious ecstasy. I've always had a capacity to see these things as symbols, as something deeper.'

This beer symbolism struck me as a shade obscure. So I stayed with the Catholicism of his youth. It seemed, I said, to have been a pretty miserable sort of religion, having to do chiefly with eternal punishment for trivial offences?

That, he said, was Irish Catholicism. The Irish were the truly Catholic people and they should probably have the Pope in their midst. The kind of Irish Catholicism which was imposed on his family in Manchester, and was still being imposed on people in Dublin and elsewhere, was a somewhat joyless kind of faith, very puritanical and scared of sex:

'When I went to live on the continent of Europe and I saw Catholicism of a different kind, in Italy and indeed in France, I saw that it was essentially not puritanical. But the priests trained at Maynooth in Ireland who came over to England did bring with them this terrible fear of sex. And this conviction that sex was a diabolic creation did, in fact, upset us at a very early age. It has been so difficult, even in late life, even at my advanced age, to overcome totally the notion that sex may be sinful. This is madness, but there it is – we can't always conquer our early conditioning. This is what really was wrong with north-western Catholicism and probably still is . . .'

Sixty years on, he still retains his early conception of God as not a very pleasant one:

'I think that God is somebody out there watching you, prepared to give you the big stick as soon as he can. There is no question of his giving you love and the promise of eternal life. The punishment aspect of Catholicism was what I was brought up with and I suppose it's still there.'

Sixty years on, he still feels it is all about punishment:

'It is not about glory and about eternal rest, it is about going to hell and burning in eternal fires. I think with later generations this no longer applies. But with my generation certainly it did, and with James Joyce's generation before. In those desperate pages about hell in *Portrait of the Artist as a Young Man* – nothing has ever been seen before in literature like it or indeed since – hell is laid out in good Jesuitical fashion, with every detail presented. And this is what I was brought up on.'

Could he not throw off that image of Catholicism?

'I think one can, but with great difficulty. Probably you have to go to a psycho-analyst or something to do it. But I always felt it is something I have to do for myself.'

I remembered that he had once said being a Catholic was like being a member of an international club where the subscription was not always called for.

'I haven't paid my subscriptions. I am very much in arrears. The subscription is to go to Mass on Sundays and Holy days of obligation, and to take communion once a year. Usually at Easter. These are the minimum obligations – I suppose the maximum obligation is just the acceptance of the whole system.'

Burgess's father had come back from the First World War to discover the corpses of his first wife and daughter, Burgess's mother and sister, tragic victims of the 1919 'flu epidemic. In his autobiography, published in 1987, Anthony Burgess wrote bitterly that as a result of that event, he had no doubt of the existence of God. Only the supreme being, he said, could contrive so brilliant an afterpiece to four years of unprecedented suffering and devastation in the First World War.

'What I said in the book was probably a little too cynical. It was the way my father felt, probably at the time, and I was just picking it up from him.'

Did he himself still blame God for what happened?

'I don't know. . . . I increasingly accept – not as mere myth – that there's an eternal struggle going on between the forces of good and the forces of evil. I have no doubt that the devil exists. I'm not prepared to identify him with God, although in the Judaic tradition it is possible to do that: Satan in the Book of Job is not the devil as we know him – he is the questioner, he is the troublemaker, who is able to present himself at the throne of God; he doesn't belong to a different kingdom.'

But in the Christian religious tradition, he went on, there was a sense of opposition between two forces:

'And if we accept that evil and good are fighting each other for ever, we are brought perilously close to the Manichean position, which is really a Persian religious idea, in which the struggle goes on for ever and there is never any resolution. There is a definite malevolence in the universe somewhere; and in our history this century we have seen it thoroughly manifested, not only at Auschwitz, but in the Russian labour camps, in the violence on our own streets.'

Once he left school, Burgess read English at university. But before long, he was called up into the army for the next outbreak of world suffering and devastation in the Second World War. In the army, he learnt something, he said, 'vaguely sentimental':

'I learned that ordinary people were very good, that the man in the street, the worker, was a good type who was being terribly exploited. I came to see that there was a terrible division in English life, the product of a long, long injustice . . . It was the voice of Field Marshal Montgomery which made many ordinary British soldiers want to become Nazis. It was the clubman's voice of Winston Churchill. We were dirt.'

He never took a commission, though he became regimental sergeant major. He chose, as he puts it, to stick with the mud, not with the upper reaches of society. He admits that since the war he may have changed his mind a little about the fundamental sanctity of ordinary people:

'But that was my experience during six years of war.'

After the war, he became an educational officer with the Colonial service. At the age of forty, an event changed his life, and set him on his writing career. He was told he had an inoperable brain tumour, and that he had only a year to live. What effect did that have on him? Was it fear? A sense of freedom?

'No, it was a sense of relief that I knew when I was going to die. I mean for the most part we don't know this. I had a year ahead of me. I wasn't going to be run over by a truck or drowned in the sea.

I wasn't going to be knifed in Soho, and I was going to live for a year. And I didn't feel too bad.'

One part of him could not accept the verdict:

'It is as we all feel. We don't think much about death except as a very abstract stranger who will eventually come into our lives.'

'Was it exhilarating?'

'In a sense, it was exhilarating. Being cut off from ordinary possibilities – you know, getting a job, and living in that job until retirement – I had to do the only thing I could do to earn a living and that was to write. It wasn't a unionised job, I didn't have to be summoned for an interview. I just had to get on with the job and try to get a living from the writing.'

'And that's what drove you to write, was it five?, novels in one year to provide royalties for your wife?'

'Well, that was the idea. I'd always been told when I started writing that it was a terrible job, so difficult, you sweated blood and tears. Of course you do, I'm doing that more and more as I get older. In those days it was a great pleasure to see that writing was a job like any other – that, like the carpenter or like the shoemaker, you had your breakfast and got down to work. And I worked every day, as I still do, writing a thousand words a day. It dawned on me that you could write *War and Peace* every year if you just stuck to that schedule of writing a thousand words after breakfast.'

'Wouldn't that become a bit exhausting?'

'Yes, it did eventually become exhausting. I published my thirtieth novel this year, which is rather too much, I'm told. I have a sort of Manchester working-man's attitude to it: this is a job, this is a job you do. You don't wait until inspiration comes. You get on with it. And I've stuck to that.'

It is now over thirty years since his imminent death was diagnosed. Like Mark Twain, he could say the report of his death was an exaggeration.

Anthony Burgess's nearest thing to *War and Peace* is his epic 650-page novel *Earthly Powers*, a landmark in modern fiction in its symphonic scope and energy. Published in 1980, and ranging over the history of the century, and its moral and religious challenges, it was voted in France the best foreign novel of the year, though it failed to win the Booker Prize. Mention of the Booker Prize did not go down well:

'Oh, the Booker Prize is neither here nor there. Once we start thinking in terms of the Booker Prize, we're going to lower all our literary standards.'

'Is it that bad?'

'No it's not. What happens with the Booker Prize is something very parochial and something very middle way which in Europe would not be well understood.'

*Earthly Powers* opens with a visit to the protagonist, the novelist Kenneth Toomey, by the archbishop of Malta. He has come to request information about a healing Toomey witnessed years ago, and so help towards the canonisation of a former Pope, to whom Toomey was indirectly related. The book's portrait of that Pope, Carlo Campanati, was loosely based on Pope John XXIII, who called the Second Vatican Council in the 1960s – an event Burgess regards as a disaster. He says it debased and secularised the Church and made religion subject to fashions. The novel's opening, Burgess said, was related to his own experience of the canonisation process of John XXIII, which began when he was living in Rome. During the gathering of evidence, for and against, Burgess was called upon to say why he was opposed to the canonisation. His deposition, he says, is part of the reason why John XXIII has not been declared a saint.

The miracle in the novel involves bringing back to life a dying boy. The boy in later life becomes the leader of a religious sect in California, rather like Jim Jones who was responsible for the massacre and self-slaughter of his followers in Guyana.

'I was asking the question, "What was God doing permitting a miracle to happen, saving a dying child so that this child could grow up to become a false Messiah putting all his followers to death?" I was really presenting the great mystery – what is God, who is God, what is God playing at?'

In the course of the novel, Burgess explores a question which to him is the fundamental problem which should affect everyone, whether religious or not. This is 'Are we free?' Out of all his guilt-laden religious upbringing, the profound Christian conviction that he has carried on into his adult life is the principle that individuals are free to make moral choices, totally free.

'I don't think it matters whether we are free to choose this make of car, or this brand of cornflakes or cigarettes, that doesn't matter. We can be conditioned to the limit by advertising, and be forced by other elements to do various things against our will. But as far as moral choices are concerned, I think we *are* free, we *must* be free. I have to hold. . . . I desperately hold on to that belief that we are free to make moral choices. That if I murder somebody, it is not some devil inside me forcing me to do that, it is myself.'

The story of *Earthly Powers* is told in the first person by Toomey, a man who doesn't believe in free choice at all, a homosexual – a condition Burgess admits he doesn't really understand very well:

'I had to take a big chance in building a big novel round the character of a homosexual. Unfortunately, the book in American bookstalls is now classed as gay literature – God knows why. . . . I made this man homosexual so that he could stand outside the normal covenants that apply to normal people. God had made him a homosexual and therefore made him unable to take part in the normal moral debate which exercises Christians . . .'

For me, the most disturbing question raised by the novel was how can violence and evil be dealt with. The book includes a chapter where Carlo, then an archbishop, confronts evil in the concrete form of a Nazi officer responsible for murdering Jews. Carlo holds the man prisoner in a cellar of his own residence, talking to him for hours each day to try and convince him of the evil of his action.

'This is something we have all wanted to do. This is one of our personal dreams – finding out what is there in the soul of this kind of person which can animate him to the kind of things he does. What Carlo finds in the Nazi officer is that there is nothing there. The man is soulless: he is a mere machine, or a mere emptiness, if you like, to be filled up with whatever particular doctrine is available.'

'The shocking thing is that Carlo is driven to committing violence on the man . . .'

'Yes, it's not terrible violence. By accident, I think, his arm is broken. And it's probably not intentional. But one can imagine that to bring about a state of mind in which the possibility of evil facing good can be accepted is to put that person in a position in which he has put so many other people. I'm not saying I approve of that, but of course, in a novel, you can get away with a lot of things.

'The people who had power in the Nazi regime never really faced the moral problem at all. I could forgive – as I think my cousin George Dwyer, and his thesis subject, Baudelaire, could forgive, and as T. S. Eliot was able to forgive – somebody who chooses evil deliberately, philosophically and then proceeds to perform evil acts. But somebody who mindlessly performs evil acts is in a very different position. . . . I think probably, and this is a dangerous thing to say, the greatest sin is stupidity and most of our young delinquents are stupid.'

'But if you are stupid, can you be anything other than stupid?'

'I'm an old teacher. I have this humanistic, liberal, conceivably false, belief that stupidity is a condition that can be liquidated. I do not believe that any human soul exists that cannot in some measure be taught.

'I gather that last year BBC TV put on a film called *The Diary of Rita* in which the way a Pakistani family were treated by some East End yobs was presented in great detail. Finally, the girl makes a molotov cocktail, doesn't she, and throws it at these thugs and kills them. That, of course, is pure sensationalism. It doesn't deal with the moral problem. The existence of this kind of being, committed to destruction, pain and the rest, without any philosophical backing, is what worries me.'

In *Earthly Powers*, Carlo believes that people are basically good. His creator does not share this optimism. He thinks people are basically neutral – that they have the power of choice between good and evil; but that before they can exercise that choice they must know what good and evil are. This, Burgess says, is one of the bases of education. It underlies morality, religion and literature and indeed all the arts and life in general. It is also, he says, totally neglected. He used to lecture on this problem in America at the time when students were concerned about whether they should be involved in the Vietnam war:

'Sometimes I was told to get off the platform by the university faculty. But I said, "You must know what you are doing. You must know what is evil and what is good. Then you must choose. And you must not in any way be affected by the edicts of government and society and your own parents. You must make that personal choice between good and evil. Whether it is right or wrong is neither here nor there".'

In his autobiography, published in 1987, Burgess portrayed his own life and his own choices. One section described in frank and honest detail his own and his first wife's heavy drinking, their mutual infidelity and his humiliation. Yet despite such experience, he still speaks of marriage as a civilising thing:

'I think marriage is the fundamental, the basis of life. Within a marriage, you develop vocabulary, you develop a culture which makes sense within that very, very small closed circle. But one also accepts that it can be outrageously difficult. One of the reasons why some people have turned against Jesus Christ, why people are prepared to accept Scorsese's film *The Last Temptation of Christ*, is that Christ didn't do the most difficult thing of all – which was to live with a woman. The new view of Christ is that he should have lived with a woman, and perhaps he did. I believe that when he began his mission at the age of thirty, he couldn't have lived in Galilee without being a married man, but that's my own personal belief.'

After the death of his first wife from cirrhosis, Burgess heard her calling to him. He regards this experience as fairly common. After all, Dr Johnson, who was very rationalistic, heard his mother calling. He rejects the idea that his own experience could have been a hallucination:

'But I do believe that when you've lived with a person for a long time, you can't face that person totally. I still dream that my first wife has come back to life again. She appears fit and well and beautiful, and sees me in bed with another woman and says: "Now stop that! We're married, we're going to get back to it." This, of course, is partly fuelled by guilt.' Burgess's famously powerful memory does not ease the burden.

Guilt seems to be a constant companion. 'Some say that the business of writing too much is an aspect of guilt, that I feel I will be punished if I don't use what talent I have to the full (this is almost biblical), that a failure of love will generate guilt almost to the day of your death. I think women are less guilty than men. I think men carry the greater burden of guilt.'

Guilt has often been the subject of his fellow novelist, Graham Green. Earlier, Burgess had labelled Greene as a 'pseudo-Catholic'. Why?

'Well, this is probably a highly personal prejudice or indeed the prejudice of my class or of my cradle Catholic upbringing. I have never trusted converts. I know that some of the greatest Catholics of the Church in England have been converts – Cardinal Newman is a marvellous example. Of course, so was the poet Gerard Manley Hopkins. But I think Greene wanted to be a Catholic chiefly because it was useful from the viewpoint of his craft.' I could feel tremors coming from the direction of Antibes, Greene's home.

'When Greene wrote the novel *Brighton Rock*, just before the war,' Burgess continued, 'he presented two systems of conduct. One was based on right and wrong, which is very secular, social and not very profound: what is right one day is wrong the next. The second is based on good and evil as parts of a permanent system. In the novel, he has this young racecourse thug, Pinkie, pursued and finally brought into the hands of the police by a non-believing lady. Greene seems to say it is better to sin than merely to do the right thing. Well, this is highly dangerous. He seems to apply to sin a kind of sanctity.'

Evelyn Waugh, the other great Catholic convert and novelist, also didn't smell too sweet in Anthony Burgess's nostrils. Life in the public house in Manchester had evidently not had many links with Catholic life as portrayed in *Brideshead Revisited*.

'I don't think Waugh would have been happy to find his neighbours at Mass were an Italian waiter from Soho and an Irish navvy. He wanted to feel Catholicism was a religion for respectable people, indeed for aristocratic people. I think this makes no sense at all in terms of the kind of Catholicism I was brought up in.

'In later life, Waugh was in great agony, because of the changes made by the Second Vatican Council. He wanted permission to stay away from Mass, during the more vulgar parts of the liturgy. An aesthetic element came in, as indeed it came into my own life.'

Like Waugh, Burgess too had difficulties with the changes introduced to the Church in the 1960s by the Second Vatican Council, though he has never doubted the existence of God.

'I have never doubted at all the rationality of the faith, granted the basic premises . . . I accept the humanity of Christ and the possibility as a theory (which of course I cannot prove, but it seems to me extremely tenable) that the only way in which the sins that man has committed against God could be atoned for was by God Himself taking on the punishment. That seems to me to be wholly rational.'

'What I have only been able to doubt,' he went on, 'is the way in which God has been worshipped, the manner in which the Church in which I was brought up has been debased by the Second Vatican Council, the way in which it has ceased to be a universal Church, and the manner in which certain basic tenets of the faith have been argued over, fought over, like cats spitting.' As for the Church of England, he's been quoted as describing *that* as a cricket club where members have forgotten the rules of the game.

One of the changes that distressed him in the Roman Catholic Church was the decision to say mass no longer in Latin, but in the language of the local people.

'To give an example, my wife, who is an Italian, and therefore brought up as more communist than catholic, and I went to Mass in Malta in Valetta, and we heard the Mass in Arabic, which is, of course, what the Maltese language is. I was put off by hearing God addressed as "Allah" and hearing that Lent was now to be called Ramadan. The universality was being lost . . . In the sixties we used to have pop singer masses, yobs with guitars on the altar. Religion was becoming secularised. It became subject to fashions. And I don't think that is what religion is about. I think religion is fundamental, it is unified and it is unchanging.'

As he got older, did he find the Christian teaching of a final judgment between heaven and hell becoming more and more real for him?

'It becomes less and less what it was when I was a child. We used to believe it was going to happen some day. I believe it is happening now. I believe the day of judgment is here and now. Whether God exists to judge us or not is not the point. The god may be in ourselves – we may be doing our own judging. . . . We can use these terms metaphorically: Christ used the term the "kingdom of heaven" – it is a metaphor. I don't think it refers to a real location. I think it is a state of being in which one has become aware of the nature of choice, and one is choosing the good because one knows what good is.'

'So, as you get older, you don't fear hell?'

'I fear death . . . As you get older, you spend a lot of time wondering what exactly is going to happen at that moment of dissolution. Will there be nothing? Will there be total blackness? Or will the ego contrive to go on living? If it was suddenly revealed to me that the eschatology of my childhood was true, that there was a hell and a heaven, I wouldn't be surprised.'

— • —

# BERNICE RUBENS

— • —

Born 26 July 1928; married 1947, Rudi Nassauer, now divorced;
two daughters. Education: University of Wales, Cardiff (BA,
Hons English; Fellow 1982). Teacher: 1950–5. American Blue
Ribbon Award for documentary film, *Stress*, 1968. **Novels**: *Set
on Edge*, 1960; *Madame Sousatzka*, 1962 (film, also); *Mate in
Three*, 1965; *The Elected Member*, 1969 (Booker Prize, 1970);
*Sunday Best*, 1971; *Go Tell the Lemmings*, 1973; *I Sent a letter
to My Love*, 1975 (film, also); *The Ponsonby Post*, 1977; *A Five-
Year Sentence*, 1978; *Spring Sonata*, 1979; *Birds of Passage*,
1981; *Brothers*, 1983; *Mr Wakefield's Crusade*, 1985; *Our
Father*, 1987; *Kingdom Come*, 1989. Also writes for stage,
television and films.

# OUR FATHER?

—•—

'There are two things in writing,' said Bernice Rubens, 'a writer writes and the reviewer then tells the writer what he or she meant. And what she has managed to do.'

'Do you find that fascinating or irritating?'

'Well, I don't on the whole read the reviews. I used to, but I don't now. I know when a book is good or bad. I know when I have conned people. I know when I've got away with it. So I am not ecstatic about good reviews, and I am not depressed by bad ones. My feeling is that everyone has to earn a living – reviewers too, so let them get on with it.'

But for the first time in her career, she had rather looked forward to reading the reviews of her most recent novel, *Our Father*, which happens to be about God.

It opens like this:

Veronica Smiles was crossing the Sahara desert, minding her own business, when she ran into God. She had seen his shadow before. Or, rather, shadows. For God was a man of parts, ubiquitous, unavoidable . . .

. . . A little nervous, she attempted to smile at Him. After all, it's not every day one runs into God. She braced herself for some momentous pronouncement . . .

. . . 'Looks as though we are in for a sandstorm,' He said.

Soon God is seriously bothering Veronica, leaving messages on her ansafone, appearing in all sorts of places, in all sorts of wild, mad, disguises to get her to face what she had chosen to forget

27

about her tragic childhood in suburbia. It is a very zany, strange, funny, sad novel indeed.

'I wanted to read what the reviewers said I had written', the author said. 'I didn't understand what I had written. I really did not know what the book was about. I thought, "Well, don't worry, the reviewers will tell me".'

'And did they?'

'No. I think they found it uninterpretable. It was open to so many interpretations. But clearly it marks some kind of disturbance in me. The fact that God was getting on my nerves meant I couldn't be an out-and-out atheist – that was a worry for me.'

Bernice Rubens has a handsome, humorous face, and dark hair, is just over five feet tall, with a slightly husky voice, and was dressed, the day we called, in a grey calf-length swirling skirt and matching jacket, and black fashion boots. She immediately gives the impression of being very good – even rather racy – company.

In 1969, her novel *The Elected Member* won the Booker Prize. In 1978, *A Five-year Sentence* was shortlisted for the same prize. *I Sent a Letter to My Love* was made into a film starring Simone Signoret; John Schlesinger filmed *Madame Sousatzka*, about a piano teacher who specialises in child prodigies. She has written other successful novels, and for the stage, television and films.

She is an intriguing story teller, often opening, as one critic wrote, with 'a politely arresting premise that gets progressively more and more bizarre'. Behind the greying lace curtains, the shabby gentility of suburbia, is a world of grotesque, comic and sad characters on a journey of terror and shame; a journey in which atonement or vengeance might be discovered, hiding in a chest of drawers.

'Your books have so much pain in them. I wonder, do you find yourself weeping over them, or laughing out loud, as you write them?'

'My intention has always been to write about sad things, because, if you think of the subjects that concern me – like loneliness and despair and depression – they are all sad; but they end up by making people laugh.'

She smiled her sad, mischievous, smile.

'That's not my intention, but I don't mind if that is the result. There is something quite ridiculous about the human condition anyway. The more tragic it is, the more hilarious it might be; and I think it is that borderline that I am interested in writing on. When I manage to balance myself on that very thin edge, it works. Sometimes I go overboard.'

'But you never consciously write to make people laugh?'

'No, I never consciously write anything. I am not conscious of what I intend to say, what message, as it were, I intend to put over. I don't have that kind of consciousness, and I'm glad I don't. I think that if I did, the book wouldn't work.'

Home for Bernice Rubens is a spacious garden flat in a large, well-maintained, cream house surrounded by trees in Belsize Park, a mile or two north of London's Regent's park.

She moved into the flat a year or two ago. It has the feel of the home of someone whose young children have grown up. The floor of the hall is of polished white marble. In the sitting room, some music scores are scattered over the Bechstein grand piano, a cello lies on its side on the honey-coloured carpet. She has been playing. She has two brothers and one sister, all professional musicians (one is a concert pianist). A maroon chesterfield and other chairs face towards an elegant fireplace. The most striking thing of all are the pictures – fine modern and antique paintings and drawings displayed against the pure white walls. The window leading to the garden is guarded with an anti-burglar device.

Bernice Rubens' father would have been proud of the room and his family. A Lithuanian refugee, he arrived at Cardiff docks in 1913. He had left Russia, as many did at that time, to avoid conscription. He was sixteen.

'It was difficult enough being Jewish there. To be a Jew, and in the army, would have been impossible from the point of view of surviving.'

He had intended to join his two brothers who had already gone to America. He arrived in New York by boat from Hamburg and was there for three weeks before he realised he was not in America at all, but in Cardiff. Though he spoke Yiddish, as well as Russian, he did not speak German, and he had been hoodwinked by a ticket tout, who had given him a ticket for Cardiff but charged him for a ticket to New York.

'He was very naive. It was a terrible shock. But then there were other people who had been similarly hoodwinked, or who had come expressly to Wales. They knew each other, or got to know each other. There was a little community between them, and they all started off in a selling business that didn't involve the buyer in any outlay of capital, because they didn't have any money.'

The favourite pursuit was credit drapery.

'In other words, you would go and buy clothes, take those clothes to the valleys, and sell them for a shilling a week. And go and collect. And when those clothes were worn out, they still hadn't been paid for. And so it would go on . . . you could never make money with it unless you were Marks and Spencers, who started in a similar way. So we were never rich, but I always thought we were reasonably happy.'

'You said somewhere that for years, in Britain, you felt like a guest in someone else's home. Do you still feel that way?'

'No, I don't. I remember during my childhood, my father used to say on many occasions, "Remember, you are a guest in this country." Although he himself was naturalised, and he spoke English well, he used to hammer it into us, "Never forget that you are a guest here." It was a kind of mantra, that orchestrated our childhood for all of us. And I believed it and behaved like a guest.'

But then her father died, and things changed.

'He is buried in Wales, in Cardiff, and I felt with that piece of ground, I had a territorial right on the country. I wasn't a guest any more.'

'And so you could be critical?'

'Well, once you stop being a guest of course, you begin to be critical. You don't have to mind your manners any more, or wipe your feet, do you?'

What depresses her most now in Britain is the gap between the haves and the have-nots, which she says becomes more and more apparent. She also regards Mrs Thatcher as possibly the most philistine prime minister the nation has ever had in its history – that is, someone totally lacking in imagination. That, she says, allows no room for lunacy or for experiment.

'And she is mightily pleased with herself, and that is a characteristic I loathe in anybody. It means there is no inner questioning – no doubts, no self-doubts, no uncertainties. I think these are very important in the make-up of a character – the uncertainties that give you a certain fear, the sort of thing that feeds the imagination. And the imagination, like anything else, has to be nurtured.'

Bernice Rubens gives the impression she knows about fear.

I asked her whether she feels primarily Welsh or Jewish.

'I don't feel anything until I'm asked that question. And if I'm asked, I feel Jewish before I feel anything, anything at all.'

'What does that mean to you?'

'I think a better question, a more valid question, would be to ask someone else, "Who is she?". Because I believe that Judaism is very much in the eye of the beholder. It doesn't matter what I think I am; in the eyes of everyone else, I am Jewish.

'One of the reasons I don't fight anti-semitism is that anti-semitism – like the poor – is always going to be with us, because I feel that man has a neurotic need for scapegoating. It's a need to find someone else to blame for all his own frustrations, on a personal level, or on a community level – his being out of work, his not being as successful as his neighbour. And as long as this remains a psychological necessity among people, I don't fight it. My feeling is, "Anti-semitism is their problem".'

I wondered whether she felt the sense of being an outsider was central to being a novelist.

'Yes, I think this links up with the fact I am Jewish.'

Philip Roth's novel *Portnoy's Complaint* highlighted for her the difference between a home writer and an exiled writer.

'This Portnoy, who is the essence of virility, as it were, and was getting it up on every page in America, goes home – home being Israel. He leaves the exile to go home. And what happens? He gets home and becomes impotent. That was an interesting crystallisation of the idea that the exile for me is the great source of creative energy.'

For this reason, she says she could not live in Israel.

'I love Israel, and am deeply on Israel's side, despite the fact that Jews, too, are available to the neurotic need for scapegoating, and we can see the manifestations of it today in their colonisation of the West Bank. I don't think I could live in Israel because I might run the risk of being at home.'

She says that to be at home is to take the edge off that creative urge that she experiences in exile.

'Although most of my novels are not on Jewish themes, I

suppose I am considered a Jewish novelist, and as long as I feel a Jewish novelist, I will feel rootless outside Israel. I think the rootlessness is the creative source, frankly. I am grateful for it.'

In 1983, Bernice Rubens published a novel, *Brothers*, which faced her Jewishness head on. It is the only one of her books in which her primary concern has been to put over a message.

'The message to anti-Semites was, "Jews are here to stay. We are a chronic permanence, whether you like it or not, and we will be here this year, next year, and every year to come".'

It is a 500-page historical folk saga of the survival, against incredible odds, of four generations of a Jewish family – from the cruelties of Tsarist Russia in the 1820s, to Wales, to Hitler's Germany, to Russia again and the modern dissident movement, and finally to present-day Israel.

She came to write it because she was concerned about Jewish refuseniks in Russia, the psychiatric abuse and so on (these were pre-Gorbachev days). She was reading the memoirs of Alexander Herzen, who was the chronicler of the times of Tsar Nicholas the First.

'In them, he wrote that the enemies of the Tsar were punished by being put in lunatic asylums. This was in 1820–25. And I thought, "Nothing has changed, absolutely nothing".'

So she began to tell the story.

The year it was published, she went to Russia to meet some Jewish dissidents. After only three days, she was thrown out.

'I went with a friend who had many contacts there. We were not allowed to go into any houses, but we were able to meet them in the street, in the parks, in Gorky Park, Pushkin Park, all the squares.'

'I know all the squares in Moscow and the parks', she added, dryly.

They were thrown out at Moscow airport, on their way to Leningrad, just told to go home.

'We were thrown out rather brutally, but that was possibly my fault because I refused to go. I can get pretty bolshie – bolshie is probably the wrong word', (we agreed it probably was, under the circumstances) 'but I felt rather bolshie in those circumstances. I refused to go without some kind of official explanation, which, of course, they wouldn't give me. So as a result, they had to send us off with dogs. It was very unpleasant.'

The year before, she had been thrown out of South Africa.

'I thought I was thrown out of South Africa, because I was writing about the women's community in Lesotho – and they didn't like it.'

*Brothers* is a deeply painful book to read. Doesn't she feel somewhere in her heart and mind and soul that the Jews have had enough of it – that it is someone else's turn to take these racist feelings?

'No, and I don't wish that on anybody, God forbid. It's been the Jews' century. But I wouldn't wish the blacks to have it. The blacks have had it too. The Indians, God knows, have had it. The gays are having it now. Everyone gets their turn. I just feel that wherever we are, and in whatever circumstances, as long as people aren't satisfied, and people never will be satisfied, people will need somebody to blame.'

In the novel, each generation passes down a litany of survival to the next generation: 'Beware of principles. Abandon them. You must if you are to survive. There is no cause worth dying for, no God worth one's dying breath, no country worth one's martyrdom, no principle worth one's sacrifice. Only in the name of love is death worthy. And friendship.'

She believes that passionately in her own life today. For instance, she never goes on protest marches on behalf of people she does not know – only for people she does know.

'But at the same time, I am very glad that people are marching, if you know what I mean. My priority is looking after my children, and not neglecting them in order to look after other people's children. It is a moral question really.'

She mentions a film called *A World Apart*, about a child she knows well, whose parents worked for the African National Congress. Part of the film crystallises the dilemma of the child, who knows she has to take a back seat to other children whom she doesn't know, but whose needs are greater. So the relationship between the child and her parents breaks down.

'I think that is a tragedy.'

In her own role as film-maker – making films for the United Nations – Bernice Rubens has travelled a great deal. No beating about the bush when I enquired what sort of films they are:

'Largely unviewable – they are in-house films about United

Nations projects in the Third World, educational, agricultural, immigrational, urban.'

She made her first film, many years ago, in Indonesia. It was about, among other things, family planning, and all forms of contraception.

'I remember I was at that time full of zeal for family planning.'

Making the film changed her mind. It also crystallised for her what she called 'the United Nations' total mismanagement with the Third World – the them-and-us syndrome'.

'I changed my mind because I realised that you don't foist your values on a people and culture that are totally different. The promotion of the pill was, "Listen lady, don't have nine children; just have two, who will survive to look after you in your old age." You can't tell that to a woman whose notion of death is quite different and whose whole culture is based on ancestry. It struck me as an obscenity to bring the pill to these people.'

The tragic breakdown of a relationship between parent and child, its results, and the suppression of those memories, is the hidden backcloth to *Our Father*, the book in which the explorer Veronica Smiles is bothered by God. God turns up in all sorts of places in a multitudinous variety of disguises. Like measles, says the author, He's all over the place and catching. Veronica wakes up one day, for instance, to find God, as superman, in bed with her. The previous night she had slept with her future husband; by morning, she is not at all sure who deflowered her. God also appears as a waiter, and as a dead-drunk orchestral violinist in a Moselle vineyard. Did the author make God appear in so many different ludicrous disguises to try and keep Him at arm's length by sending Him up?

'Well, I think, if you are afraid of accommodating a person, you have to ridicule them. That's one way of excusing yourself from accepting them. Because they are silly, or they are drunk, or they are lechers, you diminish them. I think I am diminishing God quite deliberately in that book, because I can't face him.'

'God even turns up in drag at one point . . '

'He is all unlikely things. That is the only way I can deal with it, to diminish him, to ridicule him.'

The idea of God leaving messages on the ansafone, came about like this:

'I have often come home, when I've got certain problems – nothing outrageous, usually domestic problems – and I've come in through the door, and gone to the machine, to see if there are any messages, and I think to myself, "Wouldn't it be nice, if there were a message from God telling me what to do – telling me, shouldn't I pay this bill? Or should I make a fuss about it? Should I pay the parking fine? Or should I try to get away with it?" Trivia! It is a terribly childish thing to think. I think everybody, no matter how old you are, is looking for a mother all the time, or a father, whatever the disposition of your needs. I think I am always looking for a mother.'

'How did you get going on the book?

'I don't know. The book was written, as it was written. For instance, the device of opening drawers to find letters and things, to go back to her childhood – I didn't know where it was going. It was a book in which one sentence generated the next.'

'Do you often write like that?'

'In principle, I always write like that; but I think that *Our Father* was the one that really discovered itself. That sounds terribly pseud, but I was fascinated in writing it, because the writing process was so different. I used to go to my desk in the morning, and as Veronica in the novel opens the drawer to discover the next clue to her childhood, I would go to my desk and wait for the next clue to the novel. It was incredible writing that book – I loved writing it, really loved it. I don't know whether it works. I still don't know what it is about.'

'Are you bothered by God in the way that Veronica is bothered by God in the book?'

'Not as much as Veronica. He doesn't get on my nerves as much. When I go to Israel, he bothers me – a lot of God-bothering moments in Israel. I defy anyone to go to Israel and not be bothered by God. All those reminders of Moses and Abraham and Jesus and Mohammed. It can get on your nerves.'

'Do you find that frightening sometimes?'

'No, no. I am going to be interested to know how I am going to face my own death. I'm looking forward to that. I'm not looking forward to dying – I don't think a lot about it. When I do think about it, I look forward to dying just to see how I am going to cope with it, whether I am going to let God in, because I have been keeping him out for so long. I would be interested to know if I shall die a believer. Hopefully I shall die quickly, and I won't have time.' She grins.

'Do you think you might die a believer?'

'I fear I might.'

'Why fear?'

'In principle, I don't want to believe. I think it is daft. The notion of God is daft, and I think my intelligence might be impaired if I become a believer. That's the fear. I'd sooner be intelligent, you know what I mean? I think it requires a certain stupidity to believe in God.'

She stopped, and looked across at me with a wide, amused, smile.

'What am I saying? But that's how I feel. That really is how I feel, but nevertheless, I couldn't deny the god-bothering moments in my life.'

'Why do you think it stupid to believe in God?'

A long pause.

'Perhaps stupid is the wrong word . . . If one tries to find proofs of God, it is very stupid; of course, you can't look for that kind of proof. I think that a belief in God is what people use to postpone, or even to avoid, self-confrontation. As long as you are believing in something else, you don't have to look acutely at yourself. I think that is a cop-out. I've always, much as I've disliked it, insisted on self-confrontation.'

'But in *Our Father*, God actually provokes Veronica into confronting herself, because she has to face her past . . .'

'Yes. But Veronica is a little bit like me. She is trying to get rid of God. The fact that God does make her confront herself . . .' She stopped. Then started again. 'You've just told me something about my belief, in fact – perhaps I believe in God more that I have given out. That didn't occur to me – that is an illustration, you see, of the writer not knowing what she is doing, and the critic telling her.'

At the end of the novel, Veronica acts as the 'lightning conductor' for the sins of her fathers, and expiates them. It is God who is obeyed – a God, it seemed to me, with an acute sense of vengeance. Does she think the rabbis share that view of God?

'I don't think that is particularly confined to Judaism. I think the notion of punishment and reward is pretty rampant in any creed, isn't it?'

'Well, some Christians would say that the basis to the Christian view of God is that he is offering, freely, a love to which believers respond. So, it isn't a question of demanding that we do things, because God says; it is a response to being loved. That is a fundamentally different view of God from the one of God up there demanding vengeance and right and wrong.'

'Yes, well, if I have got a belief at all, in any God, I'd sooner believe in one who is bloody-minded, who is jealous, who is full of revenge, as well as loving kindness. To me, that makes him much more human.'

'But why do you want that sort of human God?'

'The small human error makes him acceptable. In any case, what makes Judaism different from Christianity, is the notion of the chosen. Now once you have the Jews as the Chosen People, they have to be punished if they don't live up to God's choice. So you have a punitive God, and a jealous God, because wouldn't it be awful if God made a mistake? He has chosen the Jews and the Jews have to merit that choice; and if they don't, they will be punished. If they do, they will be loved.'

'There is a bit in *The Elected Member* where Norman screams at God, "Why did you choose us?". Did you choose us as a scapegoat for all your neuroses? Did you elect us to carry your wrath, omnipotence, sheer bloody-mindedness?" Was that you screaming out, really?'

'I think so – yes.'

*The Elected Member*, the novel that won the Booker Prize in 1970, centres on Norman, the clever, golden, barrister son of a Jewish family, and chosen by his relatives to carry their burdens of expectation, hope, and finally of failure and guilt as well. By the age of forty-one, he is overwhelmed by this burden, addicted to drugs, trapped by hallucinations and paranoia and eventually committed to a mental hospital. The book has an epigraph by the psychistrist R. D. Laing, who specialised in schizophrenia: 'If patients are disturbed, their families are often very disturbing.'

'I felt that said it in a nutshell – that if parents expect things of their children, they are acting out their own frustrations, their own inadequacies. Laing dealt with schizophrenics as a family problem, in family therapy. But this was a long time ago, and the Laing treatment was very much in its infancy. It was still regarded as avant-garde; now it is considered slightly old hat, and people disagree with it.'

'Did you intend the novel to have a double meaning – "the elected member" referring not only to Norman, elected by his family to carry their problems, but also to the Jewish race, chosen by God as a special people?'

'No, that wasn't my intention. That is something that has been pointed out to me by critics afterwards. I say, "Oh yes?",' (irony here), '"Well, why not?" These are not conscious things one does . . .'

A number of her novels are about people burdened with guilt, about failing to satisfy their parents' ambitions for them. Did her parents have very high expectations of the family?

'Not that I was aware at the time. I think it is part of Jewish luggage, you know. It is also part of non-Jewish luggage, except that Jews pack rather better, because Jews have had rather more hassles in packing.'

She says the Jewish religion has no notion of the hereafter.

'No cloud cuckoo land later on. If you have got something to do, you do it here and now. So there is this kind of presto living amongst Jews and I think this might account for the family expectation.'

Bernice Rubens has two daughters herself. She was married for twenty-three years to a writer and wine-merchant; but they have been divorced for several years, and she now lives alone. She says she has become addicted to living by herself.

'I am not fit to live with. In principle, I would very much like to live with someone again; but having lived on my own for so long, I would have to sacrifice too much. The price is too high.'

'You often write about people who are living alone, or are isolated or lonely in one way or another . . .'

'I think that is what I am really – a loner. One writes about oneself . . . Everything is autobiographical in a way. I am disposed towards aloneness. Not loneliness, that is a different matter.'

She says that since her marriage ended, she has never been lonely.

'Ever. When I was married, I was terribly lonely – because the expectation of not being lonely is there. You know, you have got to be married to know what loneliness is about . . . I like being with myself. But I think at the same time it is a very unnatural way to live. I think people should share lives with each other.'

*Birds of Passage* is one of the novels about people who live solitary lives. Bernice Rubens has been writing a film script for it. Set in a cruise ship, it describes a group of ageing single people, and how a rapist waiter visits two of the women at the dead of night.

'I think rape is almost as bad as murder, not to mince words. The notion of being raped and being assaulted in that way is terrifying. But I also think, because I have the kind of twisted mind I have got, I also think there might be a certain pleasure in it . . .

'In the novel, one of the widows is absolutely humiliated by it. The other secretly enjoys it. It is the first real sexual experience of her life . . .'

The inspiration for the book was a story about an American women, who was fifty-five years old, and raped. She was deeply committed to, and involved in the feminist movement in America, but when the rapist said to her, 'How old are you, anyway?', she heard herself automatically knocking ten years off her age to make herself seem younger and more attractive, even to a rapist. 'Forty-five,' she said.

One reviewer had said Bernice Rubens' books were like 'short bursts of madness, tightly controlled, and superficially logical, mingling comic horror with an appalled ordinariness.'

'Yes, I think she was being quite polite actually. Yes, I think to write is a lunatic pursuit anyway. The act of creativity is rather presumptuous, isn't it? Yes, of course I am mad, like any other writer is mad, to get up in the morning, and to face a blank page . . . and to think that the world cannot go on unless you fill that blank page is an act of lunacy. I don't mind that kind of lunacy. I'm glad I'm mad in that respect.'

'Do you think that thread of lunacy runs underneath most of the work by other novelists that you admire?'

'Yes, now that you mention it. I had not thought of it in that respect. Yes, I do. For instance, I admire Saul Bellow a great deal, and certainly, the lunacy is there. And Joseph Heller. I am trying to think of an English writer. Possibly Anthony Burgess is the only one I respect in that sense.'

In 1986, Bernice Rubens was one of the judges of the Booker Prize. 'What was that experience like – being in judgment on your fellow writers?'

'Horrendous. It is very difficult to write afterwards. Having read so many pieces of fiction, I got to the point where I couldn't read a laundry list without considering it for the Booker Prize. I read 127 novels.'

It taught her one thing.

'To win the Booker Prize is to be on the shortlist, because at that point there is some really serious discussion about books and a lot of critical analysis. After that, it is a random choice, it is anyone's guess. It depends on the disposition of the jury that year. When I won it, they were into drugs . . . I was lucky.' We both laughed.

'Is it true that success frightens you?'

'Oh, I am much happier with failure. I can cope with it. I am ashamed of what success I have. I feel guilty about it. It is just that, when I go on telly – it happened not long ago, I was on telly and someone came up to me and said, "You were on telly yesterday." I said, "No, it wasn't me, it was Beryl Bainbridge, who is a friend of mine, and we often get confused." I said, no, I wasn't, because I couldn't accommodate the conversation that would ensue. It was easier to say it wasn't me . . .

'I suppose I should go to an analyst. But the time I would spend in analysis, I could be writing another novel. And anyway, I like my hang-ups. I don't want to get better. It is not an awful thing to live with, is it? Not being able to cope with success?'

— • —

# JOHN MORTIMER

— • —

CBE 1986; QC 1966; born 21 April 1923; married: first, 1949, Penelope Ruth Fletcher; one son, one daughter; second, Penelope Gollop; two daughters. Education: Harrow, Brasenose College, Oxford. Called to the bar, 1948; Master of the Bench, Inner Temple, 1975. Member of National Theatre Board, 1968–88. Hon. DLitt, Susquehanna University, 1985; Hon. LLD, Exeter, 1986; won the Italia Prize with short play, *The Dock Brief*, 1958; another short play, *What Shall We Tell Caroline*, 1958. **Full-length plays**: *The Wrong Side of the Park*, 1960; *Two Stars for Comfort*, 1962; (trans.) *A Flea in Her Ear*, 1966; *The Judge*, 1967; (trans.) *Cat Among the Pigeons*, 1969; *Come as You Are*, 1970 (filmed 1982); (trans.) *The Captain of Kopenick*, 1971; *I, Claudius* (adapted from Robert Graves,) 1972; *Collaborators*, 1973; *Mr Luby's Fear of Heaven* (radio), 1976; *Heaven and Hell*, 1976; *The Bells of Hell*, 1977; (trans.) *The Lady from Maxim's* 1977; (trans.) *A Little Hotel on the Side*, 1984. **Film scripts**: *John and Mary*, 1970; *Brideshead Revisited*, (TV), 1981; *Edwin* (TV), 1984; British Academy Writers Award, 1979. **Novels**: *Charade*, 1947; *Rumming Park*, 1948; *Answer Yes or No*, 1950; *Like Men Betrayed*, 1953; *Three Winters*, 1956; *Will Shakespeare: an Entertainment*, 1977; *Rumpole of the Bailey*, 1978 (televised; BAFTA Writer of the Year award, 1980); *The Trials of Rumpole*, 1979; *Rumpole's Return*, 1980 (televised); *Regina v. Rumpole*, 1981; *Paradise Postponed*, 1985 (televised, 1986); *Summer's Lease*, 1988. **Travel**: (in collaboration with P. R. Mortimer) *With Love and Lizards*, 1957. **Autobiography**: *Clinging to the Wreckage* (Book of the Year award, Yorkshire Post), 1982.

# PARADISE
# UNPURSUED

— • —

'No, I certainly did not mistake my father for God', said John Mortimer, playwright, novelist and Queen's Counsel. 'And I think it was one of his great advantages that he did not mistake himself for God either. The wonderful advantage of my father as opposed to God is that my father never told me right from wrong. That's something I still don't know and have remained in ignorance of.'

He chuckled. And somewhere in the garden, I thought I heard another man chuckle in approval. A blind man in a darned tweed suit and a damaged straw hat, with a cloudy malacca cane walking stick, wandering out to do battle with the earwigs attacking the dahlias.

John Mortimer's father died nearly thirty years ago.

At sixty-six, Mortimer still lives in his father's white house in Buckinghamshire. It stands, with its green tiled roof and yellow painted window frames, surrounded, as if for protection, by an enormous garden. To get there from London, you turn off the M40 at Exit 5, make for Christmas Common and splash your way down increasingly narrow country lanes, past the village pond and village green and comfortable detached houses with names like Tumblewood and White Gables that delight the hearts of estate agents. Then, it's beyond the pub at Turville Heath and down and up the hill.

It was a still, grey autumn day. Starlings were calling in the woods and mosquitoes circling beneath the damp branches. A light drizzle made the day gloomy. Behind a thick beech hedge, the house stands hidden from the road. A red Mercedes ('Y' regis-tration) waits in the pebbled drive, the link to the Maida Vale London flat, where the family (second wife, two daughters) are spending the week. He has been left behind to get on with his writing. The visit of a BBC producer, engineer and interviewer seems like an eminently reasonable excuse to postpone the serious effort for yet another couple of hours.

In the family kitchen (wellington boots piled up by the door), he makes some fresh coffee, and then he leads us to the guest bungalow, next to the house his father built, and the conservatory added by Thames TV for the filming of his play, *A Voyage Round My Father*. 'I thought the actors and crew caught it very well', he said, 'though they did wall up some of the books in my study for two months during the filming.'

One reason why his father was so great influence on him was that he was an only child. They spent a lot of time together, and when his father went blind, he read to him. 'That's something Robert Runcie and I have in common – his father was blind too. I really began to write in order to have something to read to him. He never offered me any advice at all. He told me not to smoke opium because Coleridge had smoked it and it caused him to have terrible constipation. That was really the only bit of practical advice I can remember him giving me.'

I wondered whether he had ever wished his father had given him more advice. No, he said, he didn't. But when the war arrived and he didn't know whether to be an RAF pilot or a conscientious objector, his father suggested he should avoid the temptation of doing anything heroic.

'Well', I said, dimly remembering these and other anecdotes from his autobiography, *Clinging to the Wreckage*, and his first marriage to the writer Penelope Mortimer, 'your father didn't seem averse to advising your first wife not to marry you . . .'

'Yes', he said, quite unperturbed. 'That was a sound piece of advice also. But he was distinctly unreligious, and he believed in Darwin and Bernard Shaw. And evolution had smote him when he was at a tender age. One of the things that I admired him for was that although he became blind, so the end of his life was spent in darkness and you would think in a sort of dismal way (although he was always laughing at jokes), it never caused him to turn to God. I admired that.'

As Mortimer readers will know, Mortimer senior went blind one day when he was pruning the apple trees. He hit his head on the branch of a tree and the retinas left the balls of his eyes. He carried on with his successful legal career as well as he could, with his wife reading out briefs to him on the train up to London – on adultery, cruelty and wilful neglect to maintain. Neither he nor his wife ever referred to his blindness at all. In the play he's portrayed alternately pondering loudly on how the evolution of the horse certainly took longer than any seven-day nonsense, and raging at the family for offering him a runny egg at breakfast. The next moment, he's happily singing:

> 'She was as beautiful as a butterfly,
> and as proud as a queen
> Was pretty little Polly Perkins of
> Paddington Green!'

Members of the audience with no filial ties might be forgiven for wondering whether Mortimer senior was not only immensely self-opinionated, but given to using his calm and self-sacrificing wife rather like a much-loved doormat. What did she think of having her extremely private life revealed so publicly to the world?

'She hated it, and thought it was absolutely awful. She thought I should never have done it. It was terrible; it was disgraceful to mention our family in public. But she came from that very reserved tough middle-class ladylike kind of world in which any sort of self-exhibition was absolutely appalling, which I think it probably is.'

So, does he now regret having written the play?

Not at all. 'If you're a writer, that's your way of life. It's a sort of curse. It's particularly a curse to anyone who happens to live with you, because sooner or later, they are bound to find themselves in a book. Life for a writer has, I think, a different quality of life from anybody else because you're undergoing experiences and putting them out again in the form of some sort of art – hopefully. So you never keep your experiences. That's in a way the sad thing about my father and that play.' His round face saddened behind the glasses.

'Other people have still got their fathers, but my father has gone off to the public domain. He's acted and he's read and he really doesn't belong privately to me – that's the only sad thing. But I think that's an inevitable part of being a writer.'

To me, it seemed to me a terrible price.

'It is. It is . . . There are other rewards. The other rewards are that nothing ever happens which isn't useful to you and interesting to you and you never stop working.'

I wondered uneasily where else this interview might reappear.

In the garden, birds are singing (providing FX and atmos, as a radio script would put it). Our host is much taller than I expected. I'd imagined a smaller, rounder more untidy man, benevolent, but harassed. Someone had described him as looking like a benign, but ill-kempt pasha. Today, he's tanned, even elegant in white cricket sweater, shirt and flannels.

'You first began to write scripts when you worked for the Crown Film Unit during the war, making, in effect, propaganda films?' I enquired, treating him, in the way radio interviewers do, as if he were suffering either from senility or total amnesia.

'Yes, exactly', he confirmed kindly, for the sake of the millions we both hoped might eventually be listening.

I admitted I couldn't imagine him doing propaganda films.

'I couldn't imagine me doing it anyway. But I got the job of fourth assistant director, that's a very unimportant, sort of making-the-tea and helping-the-director job. I was supposed to have to say, "Quiet please!" at the beginning of every shot. I was terribly nervous, you know. I would say, "Quiet please!" in a very humble nervous voice, and they all went on making loud hammering and playing pontoon. And then I yelled at them, "Quiet please, you bastards!" And they all went on strike. The people in the crowd said, "You're clearly a disaster as a fourth assistant director, so you'd better become a script writer." And Laurie Lee was the script writer and I will always be grateful to him because he told me how to write a script, and then rapidly left. And so I had that job and learnt how to write film scripts. This was my war work. I wore a uniform with "Script Writer" written on it.'

Soon after the war, he took on another, rather more elevated but possibly even sillier, uniform – that of the bar. In his study, alongside family photographs and a bust of Karl Marx, are several cartoons of him rigged out as a barrister with wig and gown. His father had very much wished him to be a barrister, though was disappointed in his choice of criminal work, preferring himself the Probate, Divorce and Admiralty division of the High Court.

Eventually, after many years, he gave up his work at the bar to leave more time to write. Looking back, did he wish he'd spent rather more of his life writing than in the law?

'Well, I was always writing, starting from the time I wrote my first novel, which was published when I was twenty-three. So in a way, the barristering did not stop me. There were times in the sixties when I used to sit in long cases, when I used to write sketches for the BBC TV satirical series *That Was the Week That Was* underneath my exercise book. But it's something that's very hard for me to tell. I think I stayed a barrister too long. But if I hadn't been a barrister, I wouldn't have written *Rumpole of the Bailey* and met some charming murderers and some exceedingly nasty judges.'

I wondered whether being an advocate, and arguing a particular case, wasn't completely different from the writer's stand of being an observer.

'Absolutely. The thing about being a barrister is that you're never yourself. You're always someone else. You're always your client – a kind of mask for your client. A sort of puppet on a string. And you try and avoid the truth coming out if you're a defence barrister. You think of all sorts of artful dodges to stop that happening. Whereas if you're a writer, you have got to be totally yourself. You have got to expose yourself exactly as you are. And you have got to try and find the truth – the work of a barrister and a writer are diametrically opposed as far as that's concerned.'

I thought of A. N. Wilson's remark in his biography of Tolstoy that an essential ingredient in the psychology of many novelists is a passion for being the person who obsesses them. That seemed to be nearer Mortimer's advocate than a writer. I asked him whether he had found it useful and helpful psychologically to live in two worlds – the world of the law and of the writer.

'Well, it was very helpful in some ways. It was very helpful because I got to know a lot of people in very intimate ways. I mean, when I was very young, about twenty-four, my marriage was in a terrible state. I used to leave home after terrible rows with my wife, bleeding at the nose, my shirt torn. My car was stolen, I had to thumb a lift to the Temple. Our au pair girl was pregnant and left home. All these awful things were happening. Then I used to sit down and 60-year-old company directors would come and tell me about their problems. And I would sit there and give them the most wonderful advice on how exactly they should conduct their married lives.'

We both laughed a lot at the hypocrisies of professional life. Then he went on: 'That was very good training for a young writer. I got to be totally unshockable and I got to know an awful lot about an awful lot of people, and not only about their circumstances but how they spoke in moments of crisis. So that was very valuable.'

'When you interview people for newspaper portraits, people like Lord Denning, or Boy George, or Norman Tebbit . . .'

'Or several bishops . . .', he added with a touch of relish.

'. . . that's a different skill again? The journalistic one?'

'Yes, but I think a cross-examining technique is useful for that. My father was a very, very good cross-examiner and he used to say that the art of cross-examination is not the art of examining crossly. What you have got to do is to win the confidence of the witness, lead them gently into exposing their worst secrets. If you wish to write a hostile interview of anybody, the way to do it, is to allow them to do it themselves.'

'Of the people you've interviewed, who impressed you most or who was the most interesting?'

'The most interesting I think was Enoch Powell – because, as I'm sure you know, if you interview someone (maybe this is happening now) and they don't say anything at all dotty, strange or peculiar, then you feel very disappointed. And he did say this wonderful thing about music, how he'd liked it when he was young, but he never played it now. So I said, "Why don't you ever play it now, Enoch Powell?" and he said, "Because it doesn't do to waken unfulfillable desires", which I thought was wonderful, and a sad thing to say, and you know . . .'

He paused for a moment. Then brightened.

'When I interviewed Lord Hailsham. I said, "What do you do when you are terribly bored on the woolsack and you can't stand it?", and he said, "I mutter bollocks to the bench of bishops." Once, you know, he'd admitted he whispers bollocks to the bench of bishops, you know you're OK. The only person I interviewed who was quite unquotable was Michael Heseltine. I went home and I found I had nothing to write. So they fixed up for me to go and see him again and I talked to him some more, and I still had nothing to write.

'I really like bishops best of all. I like doing religious interviews, I really do, and I liked Cardinal Hume very much. I thought he was a very impressive and probably a very religious man. And I have got a soft spot for the Bishop of Durham, and I have this horrible sneaking affection for Norman Tebbit – he's got an awful sort of sardonic sense of humour – but I think I have grown out of that since his attacks on the BBC.'

Norman Tebbit didn't seem a specially fruitful path to pursue, so I asked him why he had such a soft spot for the Bishop of Durham, whose questioning of the traditional interpretations of the Resurrection and Virgin Birth, not to mention the views of the Blessed Margaret, had so shocked some of the faithful.

'Because he tries so desperately hard . . . you sit with him and his little feet fly in the air, and he just thumps his forehead, and he is really struggling to achieve some sort of a truth, which I think is very touching, and I think everyone's got the Bishop of Durham quite wrong. I think he's really a very devout man. What he says that shocks everybody is probably a cliché in theological schools where he comes from. And then he told me there was only a cigarette paper between my beliefs and his, which at the time, I thought was quite flattering, and then I went away and I thought, well perhaps I don't want there to be a cigarette paper. I want there to be a great gulf, you know, which I would have to leap over.'

'Why do you want the gulf?'

'Well, because in a way, to have faith in God, which is something I occasionally feel I would like to be able to have, needs a great leap in the dark, I think. It doesn't need moving across a cigarette paper. It would be for me such a total upheaval of my universe that I wouldn't like it to be so thin as that.'

'You said in that interview with the Bishop of Durham, I remember, that in some ways, you'd like to be a Christian?'

'Yes, well I think now that I'm a . . ., I'm a . . ., I believe in everything to do with Christianity, except I can't believe in God, and I don't know whether that prevents you being a Christian. I mean, some bishops seem to manage that situation all right. So that I greatly admire everything to do with the Christian ethic, but I really can't, I'm not sure that I can take God.'

'Which bishops don't believe in God?'

'Well, that's the popular thought about bishops, isn't it?'

'I don't think it's really true, though . . .'
'No, I don't either.'

Even when Mr Mortimer believes in God, he has one minor disqualification for the purple. He sees God as an incredible bastard.

'I can't understand an omnipotent god who allows children to die of leukaemia, seven million Jews to be gassed, people going to church in South America to be buried in mud and so on . . . There's a remark in the Evelyn Waugh diaries about Randolph Churchill when he was ill and had nothing to read and so read the Old Testament. He looked up and said, "Incredible bastard God was." That seems to me to be an accurate summing-up of his behaviour. I've just read the Book of Job in which God behaves appallingly. All the tormenting of poor old Job is done out of some kind of bet with Satan – and so I find God difficult to excuse, and that if God existed I wouldn't like him. I don't even find the idea of sacrificing your only son for some sort of theoretical remission of sins which you could have remitted some other way a particularly attractive way of carrying on. But once you begin saying that, saying that you dislike God, then you've got to dislike something that exists. So that you are led to believe in a god which you don't like, which is in a way a religious position, I suppose.'

'Do you find your religious views are changing all the time – or have they been fairly static for a while?'

'My views are much closer to Christianity now than they were originally. I would hate anything to happen to Christianity – particularly now in this world. I think Christianity has merged very well in this modern world. I think the bishops have stood for great good in our society. I think the Church throughout the world has been a benefit and a power for good in South America and in Africa and so on, for courage. I think I would hate for any of that to go and I would hate the village not to have a church. So therefore I'm extremely in favour of Christianity being supported. And without it, I wouldn't have any bishops to interview.'

'The main purpose of the Church being to provide bishops for you to interview?'

'It is rather like when I congratulated the jury at the Old Bailey for sitting through one of the most boring cases in the whole history of English law. The judge began his summing up to the jury. He said, "It may come as a considerable surprise to you members of the jury to know that the sole purpose of the criminal law of England is not to entertain Mr Mortimer." So probably, it is not the sole purpose of the Christian religion to entertain me and provide me with bishops to laugh at!'

'How would you describe your religious position now?'

'There are two sides to religion, aren't there? There's the side which is to do with some mystic content in the universe and there's the side which has to do with morality and ethics and good behaviour; and I think the side which has to do with morality and ethics and good behaviour is very well answered by Christianity. I think that the Christian belief in the importance of the individual person is a most enormous historical step forward and something we should absolutely cleave to – the idea that every single person is of enormous importance in the eye of eternity, is absolutely vital. So therefore I think that all the Christian ethic is vitally important. But if you then have that, without believing in God, what you're missing is a mystic reality in the universe. The nearest I can get to that is in the sort of Wordsworthian pantheism feeling about something far more deeply interfused in nature – and I can understand that. It doesn't take one very far and you can just feel a soppy pantheist.'

He looked down rather glumly. I recalled that most of the Church leaders he had interviewed had failed to answer his question about the problem of evil and pain and suffering.

'No . . . not at all . . . they never answered it.'

I had the impression they had deeply disappointed him. Maybe they should have hired him as an advocate for the defence.

Archbishop Runcie is in many ways a man rather like him. Witty. Urbane. Unsnobbish. Brave. Lurching from insecurity to insecurity. In both, cheerfulness regularly breaks in on their melancholy. But he too failed the Mortimer cross-examination.

'I didn't really get an answer from the Archbishop of Canterbury . . . I think he more or less avoided the question. Cardinal Hume told me the problem of suffering was one of the great mysteries we weren't allowed to understand. Malcolm Muggeridge told me that God was a kind of playwright, you know like Shakespeare, so he had to have the sad scenes as well as the happy ones, which I think is pretty bad luck on people who happen to be cast in the sad scenes. But the Bishop of London thought it was all ups and downs. You had to have the up and he seemed to be quite contented with that.'

It sounded as if they didn't really take the question quite seriously.

'Well, I'm sure they took it seriously, but it surprised me they hadn't all been thinking about it for a long time. But that does surprise me about interviewing people. Even if you interview politicians, you know, you ask what seem to be perfectly simple questions, like what are their political beliefs, and they say, "Come back next Thursday, and we'll think about it".'

I thought about his question about why God allows seven or however many million Jews to be gassed, and asked whether he thought he might be asking the wrong question. He seemed to be blaming God for godless actions by humans that were quite contrary to anything God wished. This launched him into the subject of free will.

'I mean, if he is an omnipotent God, a God who can control the universe, for what purpose does he allow people free will? For the purpose of adhering to him, of having the choice of adhering to him or not? That seems a kind of vanity in a way to me. I suppose the fault of that is that I'm judging God as a human being. But I find that's the only way I can judge him – as a human being. I'm not an expert in the morality of Gods. I prefer the old Greek gods who were selfish and came down and had it off with somebody instead of all this elaborate cat-and-mouse game, like giving someone free will in order that they can gas a lot of children, in order to prove how unselfish you are to give them free will in the first place.'

'But if you have children, and they behave as you wish because they don't have any choice, that must be infinitely less satisfying than having children who lovingly and freely respond by their own choice?'

'I think that's absolutely right. But are we all here in order to satisfy God's desire for our uncompelled affection? It seems, looking at it from either point of view, rather a vain conception of God – to me.'

'But what if God feels that through that method of response, the individual is most fully developed and fulfilled?'

'But you see I can do all those things – and behave well – and perhaps even do them better if I'm released from this conception. I think that the morality of George Eliot, and the morality of those nineteenth-century agnostics was really that you had to behave better and be a better person because you didn't have God frightening you into good behaviour. And the moral behaviour of Christians is certainly no better than the moral behaviour of non-Christians. As with northern Ireland.'

I was slightly puzzled by this idea that people become Christians because they are so terrified by a bullying God who hits you over the knuckles if you don't keep all the rules. I said I thought Christianity was about responding to being loved, and that was completely different.

'Yes, but I think the great virtue of Christianity, like the virtue of the plays of Shakespeare, is that whatever you want them to be, they are, aren't they?'

'Christianity,' he went on, 'is whatever you want it to be. If you want it to be what you want it to be, then it becomes as near to decent, clean, living agnosticism as it's possible to get, I think. So you can either add or subtract the concept of God at will.'

He said he had once interviewed Graham Greene and he thought his devout, sceptical Catholicism came as near to his own sceptical atheism as anything possibly could do.

'Greene ended up with a quotation from Browning, from "Bishop Blougram's Apology", which says that some live by faith interspersed with doubt, and some live with doubt interspersed with faith, some call the chessboard black, some call it white . . . you know. So you can take your choice. I happen to call my chessboard white (I ought to call it black, I suppose), but it's got very much the same squares as yours . . . I think.'

I asked him whether he didn't find the idea of morality really rather a boring notion compared with the Christian idea of grace – the idea that you are loved (not because of what you do, but that you are loved anyway) and that your life then becomes a response to this. I said that seemed a much more exciting prospect than mere morality.

'Well, I think that's an awfully difficult question which needs an awful lot of thought. The word morality can be indescribably boring; I mean, morality in the sense that Mrs Whitehouse would use the word is so boring it hardly bears thinking about. And if morality is a hard code of conduct which does not admit of any exceptions and is applied rigorously, then of course it is totally stupid and often immoral and nearly always unkind. But if what you mean by morality is what I take to be the Christian ethic that we must love one another – that every single individual is of huge importance in the eyes of the universe and therefore we must conduct our society on those ethical bases and that our own ethics must mean that we don't do unnecessary harm to other people and that we're not selfish, and we're not dishonest with ourselves or with other people and so on – then I think it isn't boring. I think that is quite hard and exciting, and it is forever exciting to produce a society which has those values at heart. Which is why I think to produce a society which is run on a monetarist basis is boring and sordid and squalid and tedious.

'Now the idea of grace, which is a very beautiful idea and particularly beautiful in the way you've put the question, depends, I suppose, on the existence of God, because you can't believe in Christian grace unless you believe in the love of God. If you don't happen to believe in a god, I suppose that's one of the finer advantages of life which are beyond me.

'But', he added, 'I certainly believe that in your personal life, of course the people you love – good, bad or indifferent – you love them however they behave.'

I said that I thought one of the differences between morality and loving, was that morality implied 'ought to', which seemed second-rate compared with loving. It was something you fell back on when for one reason or another you found it hard to love.

Yes, he said, he supposed morality was a very degraded word, but he thought the good in society could come from a kind of idea of decency which wasn't necessarily to do with love: the idea that life should be decent and honourable and fair. There are a lot of people he found it very difficult to love, but he would like them to be treated fairly. He wouldn't like them to be treated unfairly. Actually he wouldn't even like a lot of judges to be treated unfairly. He laughed.

'I think Oscar Wilde had a very good basis for socialism. You know he said that the great advantage of a socialist state was that it would save the frightful bore of having to feel sorry for everybody all the time. I think actually that's quite good. You can get on with your life, you don't have to go round loving the poor or anything, because they are being well looked after.'

At this point an electric whine appeared over the beech hedge. The engineer stopped recording until the noise faded away. 'Is this all right?' Mr Mortimer asked, diffidently. 'Yes', we reassured him. 'It's all right.' More coffee.

Judges, it seemed, were not his ideal companions for eternity. But since he had spoken of fairness, I wondered whether he ever longed for the idea of God as judge? As the Celestial Lord High Justice, togged up in wig and robes?

'I can't bear human judges. I certainly could not stand a celestial one. I think judgement is one of the worst weaknesses of human nature. If we could get away from judging people, I think we would be infinitely better off.'

I commented that he seemed forgiving by nature, and always seemed to stand back from judging the people he interviews and also the characters in his novels.

'Yes, I hope so. I hate judging. I would never be a judge. I think it's extraordinarily bad for people to be judges. They become quite extraordinarily intolerant. There is a terrible disease called 'judgitis' which they get very rapidly and they become ill-tempered, impatient, intolerant and sound off with ludicrous sorts of generalisations about human behaviour. And I don't think judging is at all interesting. When I write book reviews, I never really say whether the book is good or bad, because I think that's the least interesting thing about it. And I certainly try not to judge characters in books.'

'When you were a barrister, did you not have any moral difficulties when you knew you were defending someone who was obviously guilty?'

'No. This is a question which everybody asks barristers who defend people. The answer to it is always very simple and clear to barristers, and very difficult for ordinary people to understand. I think the first thing to understand is what a criminal trial is in England. A criminal trial in England isn't an exericise to discover the truth – it is a contest in which the prosecution has to prove guilt beyond reasonable doubt. And the defence has to argue that guilt isn't established beyond reasonable doubt. Now the fact that the prosecution failed to prove guilt beyond reasonable doubt doesn't mean at all that the person isn't guilty – they may well be guilty. It is bad enough for guilty people to be shut up in prison, but for innocent people it is absolutely intolerable.'

In John Mortimer's *Rumpole of the Bailey* novels, these dramas of good and evil, of judgement and mercy, are played out in the comic dress of human misunderstandings and absurdities. The language has echoes of P. G. Wodehouse and Evelyn Waugh.

'Evelyn Waugh was a great innovator of dialogue – with P. G. Wodehouse. It's all dialogue which is never on the point really, like overheard conversations which you cannot make sense of. And nobody ever answers anybody else's questions, which is what happens in life. If you listen to two people talking – particularly people who have been married for forty years – they never ever listen to what the other person's saying.'

Mortimer reads more poetry and history than contemporary novels. When he's writing a novel, he likes to concern himself with another art – maybe by visiting the opera or going to see a picture. What he does like very much is having a big audience, and an audience with a big spectrum. He loved it when he used to go to court and the judge and the man in the dock had both seen *Rumpole* the night before, and they had all liked it.

He can't imagine life without writing. He says it can be torture, but if someone said tomorrow, 'You're not allowed to write another word', he doesn't know what he'd do. He writes every day, wherever he is, in all circumstances. He never has a holiday.

In the sixties and seventies, Mortimer gained a certain amount of fame or notoriety through his work on anti-censorship trials. He defended the publishers of *Oz* magazine against a charge of obscenity. He defended the book *Last Exit from Brooklyn* and the lesbian novel *The Love That Dare Not Speak Its Name*. And he defended *Gay News* in the case for blasphemy brought against it by Mrs Mary Whitehouse. Is he still opposed to any form of censorship whatever?

'Well, I'm very grateful I'm out of that sort of controversy now. I feel I've done my bit in the battle, and I don't feel I have to go on with it. I hated pornography. When I had to go and see blue movies, I had to take my glasses off, otherwise they would have put me off sex for the rest of my life. But, thinking about it as well as I could, I came to the conclusion that the dangers of censorship are worse than the dangers of freedom in that respect. And that it's impossible to frame a sensible law; it's impossible to frame a law which doesn't prevent *King Lear* or artistic expression – really it is impossible to frame a law which makes any sense at all and which doesn't make the law look ridiculous. Any sort of censorship law, I think, can be used and is used by governments not to suppress things which they think are too sexy or too vulgar or whatever, but to suppress things which they find politically undesirable. So I think that the dangers of censorship are worse than the dangers of free speech.'

I remembered that when he had interviewed Malcolm Muggeridge, Muggeridge had told him that the fallacy of the liberal mind was to see good in everything.

'I don't think that that is a particular fallacy. And I think if you are a Christian, you should think that a rather desirable thing to see good in everything. I go and interview people I have been meant to do a terrible hatchet job on and I even find a sneaking affection for Norman Tebbit overcoming me! If that be a fault I would plead guilty to it.'

John Mortimer is now working on a sequel to *Paradise Postponed*, the novel and TV series which re-examined the state of English rural and political life since the war, through the story of Leslie Titmuss, who turns, not only the tables but the wardrobe, gas stove and kitchen sink, on the upper classes who despised his working-class background, and climbs his way up the social ladder to become a wealthy Cabinet Minister.

'I'm quite rude about the Conservatives, but I'm very rude about the rich left-wing people as well. So I set out to be as rude about my own beliefs as I was about anyone else's.'

'Yes, the rector comes off pretty badly. His CND marching ideals seem to change not very much and nobody in particular.'

'But I don't think you should judge anybody's beliefs by their behaviour. I don't think the fact that such a lot of Christians have been so horrible should be held to the account of Christianity. And I don't think the fact that the rector, who is meant to be a socialist and an egalitarian, is a bit back-sliding should undervalue those beliefs.'

'What was the paradise you imagine has been postponed?'

'The paradise was the paradise we were promised after the war. You know, the paradise offered by the Labour landslide of 1945 that we were going to have a society in which unemployment did not exist any longer, rich and poor wouldn't exist any longer . . . there would never be any more Conservatives. We would all enter into the just city – I mean, whether that's a paradise anyone particularly wants – perhaps it isn't? And I think it's in the nature of people not to want paradise – I think they like a little bit of evil round the place.'

'What is the paradise you want?'

'Well, I don't want paradise, certainly. I think paradise would be unbelievably tedious. That's why I don't want to have immortality. My father said what a terrible idea it would be, like living in a huge transcendental hotel with nothing to do in the evening. What I would like is to live in England as it is with a little bit more social justice, equality and reasonable treatment of everybody. It wouldn't be paradise, it would be better.'

'The book, I suppose, highlights two different ways of looking at the world. Is it better to hope for paradise even if it's unattainable? Or to accept that life is nasty, brutish and short and go out for self?'

'I believe totally in the first view. I think, too, that is a good thing to think about religion. . . . If you act on the assumption that we're all nasty, brutish and short, and you had better make as much money on the Stock Exchange before the crash comes, it's not going to be a very pleasant world.'

'You've spoken of Britain's present "Bizarre religion of greed".'

'Yes.'

'That's quite a strong attack on Britain today.'

'I think it's a pretty disgusting situation, the idea that money is the entire be-all and end-all of existence, that everything is judged now by whether or not you make money. People are meant to be educated now simply in order to make money. The idea that you are educated in order to be a more tolerable person, or to lead a richer life, when you are sitting by yourself, has totally gone. That was the thing I was always trying to write about in *Voyage Round My Father*, trying to write about it always – in the mother in *Paradise Postponed*, and *Rumpole* too. Money was meant to be not only totally uninteresting, but something which was quite slightly disgraceful to have – and I think that that was quite a healthy attitude.'

'But isn't it only people who can afford to have that attitude who think like that?'

'Of course, certainly, and that's again what *Paradise Postponed* said. But the awful thing is people who've got the money, and then proceed to think it's important and that they need to get more of it.'

'Were you upset by the *Daily Telegraph* attack on you accusing you, round about the time of the broadcast of the TV series, of hypocrisy and of posing as a moralist, and claiming you were a champagne socialist, living in wealth?'

He stirred in his chair. 'That's also something that's said of us when we try and have different political aims from those of the present government. But I think it is totally ludicrous. Is there a kind of income level, is that what the assumption is, that there's a sort of income level, at which you can no longer be allowed to believe in a fair distribution of wealth? I mean, it's OK to be a socialist when you're earning £10 000 a year, but when you're earning £20 000 you have to automatically vote conservative? I think that's the most ridiculous idea. Nobody ever said to Bernard Shaw that he shouldn't be a socialist because he was a millionaire. All social change has been brought about by members of the affluent middle classes, and unless the people who've got money are going to be concerned about the poor, I don't know who is going to be, because that's what they want, what the Conservative people would like. They would like only the poor to be interested in the poor and the poor wouldn't be effective in arguing the case. So it's really a part of saying, "All shut up, and let us get on with it".'

'What's to happen now to the Right Honourable Leslie Titmuss?'

'In preparing myself to write that, I started with reading the Book of Job.'

'Why Job?'

'I haven't quite worked that out yet. I'm sure it's going to be important. I don't know yet whether Titmuss is God, Satan or Job. I have a horrible feeling he's God.'

'Will you find out in the course of the novel, or do you plan it fairly carefully beforehand?'

'No, no, I don't really plan it now. You should know what the theme of the book is, I think, and you should know where you're going to, hopefully. But I don't think anything is good unless it surprises you – unless you can create characters which will do something you didn't expect they were going to do, they're sort of dead. It's a great dilemma. You've got to create the characters first and then find out what they are going to do. I remember when the TV series of *Paradise Postponed* was planned, actors were hired, the director was there, and I still had no idea how the novel was going to end. It was very nerve-wracking, but it did end.

'It's very interesting', he went on, 'if you read Dickens' notebooks on *Little Dorritt* for instance. You'd think that from the beginning he'd have the idea that the second half of the book would be the Dorritts getting rich. But the whole thing had been published in parts until about half way through, and then suddenly he writes a note to himself, saying, "Well, what a good idea it would be if the Dorritts became rich".'

'He had the same problem with *Bleak House*, didn't he? It was being published in parts, and then it was moving towards one ending, and then he ditched it.'

'Yes, that's right, that's why they're good, because the people are alive and they're not going to do what Dickens tells them to do. They'll do what they want to do.'

'You once said that a deeply pessimistic view of the human condition was a recipe for a happy life . . .'

'Yes. Well, I don't believe in immortality, therefore I believe that life is very short, a ludicrously short period, so every minute is very precious. I also think it's very important not to expect too much. Then you get pleasantly surprised.'

He who expecteth nothing will not be disappointed.

'All my clients', he went on, 'that I ever appeared for, I've always told them you know, that the case was going to be a disaster, they'd probably go to prison for ten years, and so on, and you know, they get fined five bob, and they are absolutely over the moon. I think it's a very sensible way of proceeding.'

During his own interviews of the famous, he nearly always asks them if they think much about dying. Does he himself think much about dying?'

'Yes. I do. I find it very, very irritating, and, you know, I can resent it deeply, but I suppose there's nothing very much to be done about it.'

— • —

# PIERS PAUL READ

— • —

FRSL; born 7 March 1941; married 1967, Emily Boothby; two daughters, two sons. Education: Ampleforth College, St John's College, Cambridge (MA). Artist-in-residence, Ford Foundation, Berlin, 1963–4; sub-editor, Times Literary Supplement, 1965; Harkness Fellow, Commonwealth Fund, NY, 1967–8. Member, Council, Institute of Contemporary Arts, 1971–5; Committee of Management, Society of Authors, 1973–6; Literature Panel, Arts Council, 1975–7; Adjunct Professor of Writing, Columbia University, New York, 1980. **TV plays**: *Coincidence*, 1968; *The House on Highbury Hill*, 1972; *The Childhood Friend*, 1974. **Radio play**: *The Family Firm*, 1970. **Novels**: *Game in Heaven with Tussy Marx*, 1966; *The Junkers*, 1968 (Sir Geoffrey Faber Memorial Prize); *Monk Dawson*, 1969 (Hawthornden Prize and Somerset Maugham Award); *The Professor's Daughter*, 1971; *The Upstart*, 1973; *Polonaise*, 1976; *A Married Man*, 1979 (televised 1983); *The Villa Golitsyn*, 1981; *The Free Frenchman*, 1986; *A Season in the West*, 1988. **Non-fiction**: *Alive!*, 1974; *The Train Robbers*, 1978.

# A MARRIED MAN

— • —

'There was a survey in the paper, not long ago, about marital infidelity', said Piers Paul Read, for years the pin-up author of female editorial assistants in certain literary publishers. 'It found that women are much less faithful than they were ten years ago, and much more quickly unfaithful than their husbands. The reasons many of them gave were the reading of the novels of Margaret Drabble and Fay Weldon.'

He looked rather amused and a shade shocked at this astonishing piece of information.

'I suppose I like to hope that if Margaret Drabble and Fay Weldon can influence people one way, I can influence people the other way.'

I had asked him whether novel-writing did any good. We were talking in a sitting room of his elegant five-storeyed white house on a quiet residential street in London's fashionable Holland Park. Bicycles, a table, and tennis rackets littered the front hall. Then it was through the light, spacious open-plan kitchen and down the steps to the lower-ground floor. There were deep settees, a grand piano, a Georgian-style doll's house, a wicker basket full of toys, a complete set of the *Encyclopedia Brittanica*. Modern paintings, tasteful watercolours, and chalk drawings hung on the walls. One wall was lined with novels. Lamps were ready to cast a warm, soft light, when the evening drew in. It was a family sitting-room of the cultured English educated classes. Except for one thing. A portrait of the Pope stood on the mantelpiece.

Charming and diffident, Read was wearing well-cut grey trousers, and jacket and a blue shirt; but he has an air of a monk about him. A tall, thin, ascetic figure, with brown eyes and an ironic, mischievous smile hovering round his lips, I could have imagined him in a black habit – one of the English Benedictines, say, who taught him as a child.

At the age of eight, he was sent away from home – first to a Catholic prep. school, then to Ampleforth, where Benedictine monks educate the children of the wealthy, Catholic upper-middle classes. He did not like it at all.

As in many public schools, there were monitors, and bullying and quite a lot of beating. His complaint was not that the monks wished to imprint on the boys the Catholic faith, but that they were imprinting on them instead the ethos of the British public school. He regarded this as a betrayal of their Benedictine inheritance.

'Funnily enough, a lot of the things for which I criticised them as an insolent fifteen-year-old – this sounds very conceited – they later abandoned. Ampleforth is now unrecognisable from what it was in my day – beating, bullying, the lack of culture, the idolisation of sport, and that kind of thing. I think they still think rugby is important, but I hope they don't think it is the only thing that moulds character.'

At that time, Cardinal Hume, now the Archbishop of Westminster, was a housemaster of another house. But Read only knew him slightly:

'I knew him better when he became abbot of Ampleforth. I see him occasionally now.'

'Has he been a strong influence on your life?'

'No, not really. My house master, Father Patrick Barry, who is now the abbot, was more of a figure in my life at Ampleforth. I had great quarrels with him.'

Piers Paul Read says he was sent to Ampleforth partly to propitiate a God his mother felt she had offended.

Neither his mother nor his father were born Catholics. His mother was converted to Catholicism in her late twenties in Edinburgh. Three months later, she met and fell in love with his father, who was already married, with a ten-year-old child. He was Sir Herbert Read, a respected art historian, publisher and a poet. He left his family for her.

'So we were brought up very strictly as Catholics, but with my mother being in a state of mortal sin as we kept being told, because she was married to my father who had a wife still living.'

'Technically, she was excommunicated at that time?'

'Yes, she never wanted to go to the sacraments while he was alive. She didn't think that she ought to be allowed to go to the sacraments.'

'Do you think she was right in that?'

He paused a long time.

'It's a difficult question. I think I do really, yes. She certainly thought she was. She always said, there were rules, and if you break them, you should know what the consequences are. I think she hoped that the grace of God would, as it were, save her, despite her breaking the rules. She thought love was a more excusable sin than some others.'

'Were you ever tempted to adopt your father's kind of humanism?'

'I should have been, because I adored him and admired him enormously. He was very intelligent and had an encyclopaedic knowledge of very many subjects, and worked enormously hard.'

As a teenager, he rebelled very strongly against his mother's influence, and against Ampleforth. He left the school at sixteen.

'I remember going to Father Michael Hollings, who was then giving a retreat, and saying, "Look, I can't bear this whole ethos of the school," and he, rather wisely, said, "You mustn't think that Ampleforth and the Roman Catholic Church are the same thing." So I made a distinction.'

He now puts it down to the grace of God that he did not abandon his faith and follow his father's beliefs.

One of his first novels was *Monk Dawson*, published when he was twenty-eight. It tells the story of a boy educated at a Benedictine public school, who then becomes a monk and abbot, and who later abandons that way of life. The Second Vatican Council of the 1960s, called by Pope John XXIII, had reminded the Catholic Church of the challenge of choosing what was called 'a preferential option for the poor'. Part of the book is a satire on Ampleforth, on monks choosing instead a preferential option for the rich. Finally, Dawson becomes a member of an extremely austere silent order.

'The ending of the novel is meant to be ambiguous. As far as I am concerned, he does have a real vocation as a Trappist monk and this is the will of God. It is left to the reader to decide that this might also be a sign of his insanity. But then,' he added, as an afterthought, 'from the point of view of non-believers, Trappists are insane.'

The main character in that novel is attracted for a while to Marxism. Was it true that he once said that a Roman Catholic who wasn't a revolutionary was living in mortal sin?

'Er – I don't think I said that', he said, nervously.

'You are certainly quoted as saying it . . .'

'I did go through a phase certainly of thinking that if you were a Christian, you were obliged to love your neighbour, and that the most effective way of loving your neighour was to bring about a revolution, and have a general levelling and sharing of goods. But I remember reading a book about a priest who had been in China and became very sympathetic to the revolution, who said, "I have come back a communist, but although I'm a communist, I'm always a Catholic first." And I think I was only a Marxist or socialist, because I was a Catholic, and would always have subordinated my socialist beliefs to my Catholic beliefs.'

'Did you ever think of giving up all your possessions?'

'I didn't have very many possessions to give up', he said, with a smile. 'No, I was quite interested in politics, and thought of becoming a politician, and I was left-wing . . .'

Today, he still opposes the public school system, Oxford and Cambridge, and the idea of monarchy.

At thirty-two Piers Paul Read published *The Upstart*, a novel about a young man's humiliating slights through the snobbery of the upper classes, and his criminal revenge. Hatred wells out of the book. Read says the first part of the book was autobiographical – it was the experience he went through as a child. When he was eight, his father had the romantic notion of returning to his roots in rural North Yorkshire. But by then he had become an art critic and a publisher, and was cut off from the farming folk from which he came. Yet he wasn't part of the gentry.

'At that time in North Yorkshire, there was really no middle class between those two groups of society. My mother, who wasn't even English, suffered as a result from what we perceived to be a certain amount of contempt of our social standing. That certainly gave me a hatred of the rich, and hatred of the upper classes, which in turn inspired my left-wing views . . . I think I realised, as I got older, that a lot of it came from pride and envy, and it wasn't a very genuine altruistic ideology.'

'When you create almost demonic characters like your main character in that novel, do you think it reveals to you the evil latent in you?'

'I think it would be impossible to create a character who wasn't from one's own potential. One of the reasons I would give for being grateful for faith (or a pyschologist might say, clinging to a structure), is that I'm aware of what might have been, had it not been for the grace of God.'

'Do you find it frightening sometimes to create a character steeped in evil?'

'Yes. Not so much in *The Upstart*, because I think it became slightly unrealistic . . . For instance, there's a moment, when he drowns a baby. I brought that in deliberately, because I thought he'd been rather too attractive, rather too roguish and pleasant, and I wanted to show him doing something, which everyone would agree was pretty nasty, and at the same time, make a point about abortion. I think the novels *Polonaise* and *The Junkers* – which I wrote when I was quite young, and which include some very unpleasant scenes – frightened me rather more.'

Some time after writing *The Upstart*, Piers Paul Read left London to go back for a while to Yorkshire. Was that to exorcise ghosts?

'One of the disadvantages of being a writer is you have this enormous choice as to where you want to live. We were living in London, and I felt very constricted, and we couldn't afford to get a cottage in the country, as well as having a house in London.'

Finally, he bought a house in Yorkshire smaller than, but very similar to, the house his parents had.

'It took five years for me to realise that it was a regressive move. But it did work out of my system my romantic notions about my childhood and my roots.'

Does he feel the same way about the Yorkshire gentry, as he once did?

'Well, I don't feel personally affronted by other people being richer than me, or more powerful than me, which I think I probably did when I was younger. I certainly have a certain – contempt is perhaps too strong a word – pity for people who think the whole point of life is to be richer, have big country houses or whatever, as my most recent novel, *A Season in the West*, shows.' More of that later.

*Alive*, the best-selling non-fiction account of the survivors of the Andes plane crash who had eaten parts of the dead bodies of their comrades while waiting for rescue, was a book he didn't want to write at first.

'I thought it was a disgusting story. Then the American publisher persuaded me to go out there, and I was given the job by the survivors very much because I was a Catholic, and they thought they could trust me to write the kind of account they would approve of. As I became involved with them, and relived what they went through, I realised that the cannibalistic side of it, although that was the most sensational, wasn't the most important. What was most impressive was their very, very strong desire to live.'

Read himself had no particular views whether eating the bodies was right or wrong.

'But the Church came down very quickly and said it was permissible. And that was wonderful for them . . . They came down from the mountains very troubled in conscience as to what they'd done, and almost the first person they met, a young Chilean priest, said, "What you did was perfectly right".'

That, he said, helped them enormously to get over the psychological problems.

'When I showed them the finished manuscript, they were very upset and said I'd put in "all these details", as they kept saying. And they said they would have to leave the country, because people would disapprove so much. As far as I know, they have had no adverse criticism at all. In fact, they have become heroes in their country as a result. I think people think they did the right thing, and that it was admirable, because they did it, as I hope the book shows, not for purely selfish reasons, but because they wanted to get back to their families. Very strong family feelings, they had.'

It was while he was living in Yorkshire that he was commissioned for his next non-fiction book – about the Great Train Robbery, when two-and-a-half million pounds was stolen off the Glasgow to

London train. He wrote it because he wanted to know more about criminals:

'I think *The Upstart* rather deteriorates towards the end, because it is not very convincing when the main character becomes a criminal, because I didn't know anything about criminals. And I thought, "Here is an opportunity to work with ten or eleven hardened criminals, and find out a bit more about the criminal mentality".'

The writing of it was a nightmare.

'They were having contractual quarrels with the publisher; and the only way they could exert pressure on the publisher was by not turning up at the "meets" as they called them, which they'd arranged with me. So I would come down from Yorkshire, expecting to have a session with them, and they wouldn't turn up.

'Then if you read the book, you discover they told a lot of lies. The whole project was a hoax – and I didn't find that out until much later. I had to sit down and write the book, knowing that a large part of the story wasn't true, and being thoroughly sick of the whole project and fed up with them. It was really a great test of professionalism to write a book under those conditions.'

He learned two main things from writing the book.

'First of all, an understanding not of the criminal mentality, but that the criminal mentality has many forms and you can't really generalise about criminals. Secondly, funnily enough, it made the prospect of living in London more acceptable, because I think having been brought up in Yorkshire and in the country, I was rather frightened of living in London. I really felt there was a whole seething underworld around me, which I didn't understand, and couldn't cope with. But having coped with these eleven heavies, as they were, and having mastered them in quite difficult circumstances, I really lost my fear of London, because I felt that if I can cope with them, I can cope with anything.'

'Is there any one of them you found particularly interesting psychologically?'

He searched round for a few seconds as to how to respond.

'Well, this is where I think it is difficult when you're dealing with evil. I later attended the trial of the Yorkshire Ripper, who's a criminal of a different sort obviously. Evil is very, very difficult to pin down. Whenever you try and pin it down, it jumps out, and enters into some different category. Some of the robbers, you felt, were psychopaths; others were fools; some, you felt, were cunning rogues.'

It was very difficult, he said, to generalise about what the robbers did.

'Buster, the one they made a film about, is a charming man, and had certain very fine qualities of loyalty to his friends, and it is very difficult to feel, when you are with him, that he is evil, because he's so charming. Biggs was a very charming and amusing fellow. On the other hand, you know, as I went into their backgrounds, and what they'd done, I'm sure that coshing the train driver was the least of their wicked deeds. I think they have done many worse things than that.'

I recalled that some years ago, I had watched a television interview with Pol Pot, then leader of Cambodia, and had been quite fascinated by what he was saying, and had thought, "What a very interesting dinner companion he would make." Then, several months later, the appalling stories came out of what had been happening in Cambodia – with millions of people killed. I was disturbed that this obviously evil man had appeared so apparently charming in the interview.

'Yes, but you could say that of Robespierre or Torquemada. A lot of the people responsible for what we now regard as atrocities might have appeared very charming people over the dinner table . . . That is what I try to show in my novels – that you can't categorise evil, say in a social or political way. It's much more complicated than that. And much more personal than that. That's why I believe very strongly in a personal devil.'

'Do you have a personal devil?'

'My guardian devil, as opposed to my guardian angel, you mean? Yes, I'm sure I do. Yes, the little demon whispering in my ear. I know it's very unfashionable to talk about, or appear to believe in hell, or in a personal devil, but I don't think the whole Christian concept makes sense without the existence of hell, and the existence of a personal devil.'

He says that the more he tries to look at evil, the more capricious and arbitrary it seems to be.

'In the same way, you can't really systematise *good*. All attempts to systematise good, as through socialism, usually in the end lead to evil. Evil jumps in and out of different human and historical situations – so that at one moment, the communist is a benevolent idealist, and the next minute he's building his gulags in Russia, and suddenly he's perhaps a good fellow again, as a *glasnost* exponent. You find this in Nazism too. This convinces me that there really is something very personal about evil, that there is what Jesus called "an evil one", not just evil.'

One of Piers Paul Read's novels, *The Free Frenchman*, focuses on French history in the 1930s and 1940s and during the Second World War:

'In a sense, I wrote it simply to illustrate that to say, "All Marxists are bad, and all Pétainists were bad, and all Gaullists were good, and all the Resistance were good," is not true. There were good and evil people on both sides; and you even got people who, for good motives, fought for the Nazis, because they thought they were saving Christian civilisation. I think life is full of these moral paradoxes, which one has to try and cope with.'

'Do you feel that politicians and political parties try to corner morality?'

'Yes, I do. People say I have become right-wing. I have not necessarily become right-wing, but I feel I have seen through a lot of the posturing of my earlier beliefs – a lot of what one regards and presents as altruism is really a form of envy, and is morally very simplistic. People use concepts of good and evil for their own ends.'

Piers Paul Read explored the muddiness of personal motives in a novel called *A Married Man*, which was later televised. It is the story of a successful barrister, who reads a Tolstoy short story, and realises that his life has gone completely wrong. He becomes a candidate for the Labour Party. He also embarks on an affair.

'I suppose what I feel particularly strongly about him is that people often take a high line on South Africa, or communism, or whatever, and don't see the immorality of the small details of their own life. I do very strongly believe that charity should begin at home – that people must try and be good in the context of their family, before they start moralising about wider issues.'

'You have said that to want to divorce is to want to murder. Do you really believe that?'

'I think the thought, "How much more convenient it would be, if he died", always enters the mind of people who are in the process of a divorce, because they would be saved the opprobrium of divorce.'

'What was the theme you wanted to press home at the end of the novel?'

'Belief in marriage. The hero, at the end, realises that really he loved his wife, and that marriage meant much more to him than he'd thought.'

'And that religion, not politics or adultery, is the best way to ease life's difficulties . . .?'

'Yes. There, this silly, rather vain, rather self-conscious man had been pursuing what he thought were the immediate attractions – the mistress, the career – to try and take him out of his mid-life malaise, when in fact he hadn't seen the value of the things that were under his nose.'

Read thinks that is a real problem in many people's lives:

'So many people are discontented, or think they are discontented with their wives, or their marriages, or their jobs, or the way they're living, and have silly notions about what would make them – if only they won the pools, if only they had money, if only they ran off with a prettier girl or something, or had a more handsome lover. That is the devil. That's the devil just dangling these silly illusions in front of them, and if only people would see the value of what they have, then they'd be much happier, and other people would be much happier too.'

'There's a section in the novel where you reveal letters written by a priest to the wife, who is also tempted to have an affair, and her response to them. Do you ever feel that in some ways you would have liked to be a priest?'

'Yes. Yes, I do. I don't think I was called to be a priest, but I think anyone who has been brought up by priests and has been in contact with priests is touched by the concept of being a priest . . . But I had always wanted children very strongly, before I wanted to get married, or have a girlfriend even.'

A boyish smile lit up his face.

'I remember when I was a child, when we all discovered the facts of life, with my sister and her friends, and we were discussing this appalling deed that had to be done, in order to have children, they all said, "Well, nothing will ever persuade me to submit to this indignity." Then I thought, "Well, it is a dreadful thing to have to do, but I think for the sake of having children, I'd do it.'

'You wrote some years ago that you believe the Catholic religion has a divine distaste for the erotic. You accepted then that the Church was right, and novelists were wrong. What did you mean?'

'Well, one of the problems for the novelist and for the artist is that there is really very little theology of art. I don't think that the Church has even made very clear what virtue there is in great art. It uses artists to decorate the Sistine Chapel or whatever, but it doesn't canonise artists. And then you get a novelist like Stendhal, who is a genius, I think, as a novelist, but is bitterly anti-Christian, and the whole of his novels are sort of celebrations of carnal life. Now the Church is very suspicious of carnality – of the flesh. I don't think you can avoid, as many Christians now do, the traditional mistrust of the flesh in Christian teaching. Even in revealed religion (although some of the Old Testament is very erotic – the Song of Songs and that kind of thing), the fact was Mary was the Virgin Mary and Jesus never married. St Paul said it is better not to marry. I don't think one can avoid the fact that God is showing us a mistrust of the erotic.'

I agreed that the Church has often an ambivalent feeling towards art, and that people who are known to be Christians are sometimes criticised for including in their work material that other people regard as anti-Christian. But it seemed to me that the writer has to write what he or she has to write. He agreed:

'I think if you try and make art propaganda, even for the cause of the Church, it destroys it as art. You've got to imbue it with Christian values and Christian spirit in a much less direct way. *The Upstart*, which is a novel of mine which is most carnal, does end with an actual conversion of the hero. But mostly in my novels, I show it in a less direct way.'

Read has always had a strong faith, and thanks God for it. He says he has never doubted Christian teaching or the claims of the Catholic Church.

'I don't just automatically believe what the Church teaches just because the Church teaches it, but there's never anything that I can think of that I can't stomach.

But he inherited from his childhood a certain shame at being a Roman Catholic.

'In North Yorkshire at that time, despite Ampleforth, it was always slightly embarrassing to be a papist; and I think also at Cambridge, when I was there, it was very embarrassing to say one believed in God. One was mocked by one's fellow philosophers and moral scientists for expressing such a naive belief. And I think, even in London today, people are slightly embarrassed if one brings religion into conversation at dinner parties. But I do feel, that if you're given that faith, it would be very cowardly not to state it, and to try and state it particularly in areas where you feel it's not being expressed.

Last year, he was asked if he wanted to write a piece for *The Tatler*.

'Now *The Tatler* magazine is not a magazine I would normally write for, but I thought I ought to take that opportunity. I have very much felt that the Christian case often goes by default in our society, particularly in the media or liberal London circles, and that it shouldn't go by default.'

'Do you think that having a very clear set of convictions and beliefs is an advantage to a writer or a disadvantage?'

'I think it's a disadvantage if those beliefs make his art into a form of propaganda. I know that some people think my art is warped and distorted by my religious convictions. But, I would say in my defence, that I don't think some of the people who like my novels (and this includes reviewers, as well as the general public) like them in particular because they are thought of as Catholic novels, or not Catholic novels.'

For a while, Piers Paul Read lived in Nice – not far from Graham Greene, who was a great friend of his parents, and was his sister's godfather. They once bought a pony from him.

'I think his writing and his narrative power is wonderful. There are certain things I could criticise about his work.'

'What?'

'This is rather impudent, to speak of a great writer like this, but his female characters never convince me very much. I don't believe in these saintly little prostitutes or saintly waifs that keep cropping up in his novels. I have yet to meet one.' He grinned.

His own Catholicism and writing tends to be set within the family. I wondered if he was never tempted to try wider Catholic themes, like exploring the question so many atheists ask – why a loving God can allow such immense suffering to innocent people.

'It's never a problem that has particularly perplexed me, because I have always seen suffering as a result of the Fall. The real drama of the human condition is that God has given us this choice and this opportunity to be as gods – and that suffering is a necessary consequence of that choice.' He paused. 'It is not the way I write novels really. I don't sit down thinking, "Right now, I will write a novel about suffering".'

'How do you go about writing novels?'

'I start off with some moral idea I want to illustrate. Then before I begin, I outline the plot on a single page.'

'Do you see yourself as a moralist?'

'Yes, I mean, I think my wife thinks I'm rather a sort of pulpit-bashing preacher, really. I hope I'm not too much of a moraliser, but I think it is the duty of a Christian, to some extent, to preach the gospel through whatever they do, and I think the function of a novelist, whether he's Christian or not, is to examine moral ideas, and therefore in examining moral ideas, I try and present a Christian perception of what the answer should be.'

'Do you find it difficult being a writer?'

'Yes, on several levels. It's quite difficult working alone entirely, and year after year. It is difficult having to rely on your own resources to produce ideas and works of art. I think the writer is rather a weird figure in society. He has got less of an obvious social function than in other countries.'

'Isn't there a certain *cachet* in being a writer then?'

'In France or Russia, you are rather a figure of respect. In this country, people are pretty suspicious. I think they think you are trying to skive off doing a proper day's work.'

'Maybe they are frightened you will write about them?'

'Yes. I think also it's a Yorkshire thing. Yorkshire people are very philistine on the whole. And they always took the view that writing was just a way of avoiding doing proper work.'

I laughed, and said that at this rate, they wouldn't be letting him back into Yorkshire . . .

During his time in Nice, Piers Paul Read began a novel set in the South of France, called *The Villa Golitsyn*. Its central character is a man drinking himself to death to drown his remorse for his incestuous relationship with his sister, a sin which he admits that, were he to have his life again, he would commit again. The novel explores whether or not some things are intrinsically evil, even if they do not cause suffering.

'In other words, as a brother and sister living happily together, why shouldn't they sleep together, if they are not going to have children? Is incest a sin, if no one suffers? The popular widespread conviction now is that, if no one suffers from a particular act, then there can't be anything wrong with it. The book shows a man, who although he had convinced himself that no one was suffering from this particular act, nevertheless felt that it was a sin, and that he had somehow offended God, and might be damned.'

It occurred to me that the moral dilemma had echoes of his mother choosing to continue to live with a man who already had a wife, even though she believed it placed her in a state of mortal sin.

'I hadn't thought of it in terms of my mother, but sub-consciously, you may be right. It could apply to my mother.'

'Do you completely reject the view that if people don't suffer, then a particular moral course is acceptable?'

'Yes, because I think some things are intrinsically evil. There is a phrase in Goethe's *Faust*, which says that everything material is a parable of things going on above . . . There is good and evil in acts which have nothing to do with the immediate consequences to other human beings. In other words, I think one can be a saint or a sinner on a desert island. I don't think there have to be other people around for a person to be good or evil.'

The narrator in the novel, Simon, is a diplomat who visits his host to discover whether, some years ago, he betrayed his country. By the end, the diplomat appears to be far worse a man than he is – a rather subtle development.

'Willy's remorse brings him to God. He feels remorse, and thinks, "I can only feel remorse, because I've offended a god." Whereas Simon is this practical, cold, calculating, complacent man who doesn't sense his own sin, and therefore doesn't repent, and therefore doesn't find God, until right at the end, when he's in fact touched, if you like, by the saintly sinner, who's then dead in heaven.'

Read's latest novel, *A Season in the West*, deals with a Czech dissident, who defects to London, only to discover that life in candle-lit Establishment society in Holland Park throws dark shadows. Some of it struck me as extremely funny, for instance, a scene where he is invited to lunch with some leading writers of the day, and he's looking forward greatly to asking them some intel-lectual questions about the state of English fiction; but their conversation centres exclusively on who is sleeping with whom, and the size of their advances. Does he really have a very low view of London literary life?

'Yes, I suppose I do,' he said, with a slightly embarrassed laugh after a thoughtful silence. 'That was satire, so it was slightly exaggerated, but I think there is a reluctance among writers to talk seriously about anything. They sometimes will show off a bit their knowledge of this and that, but I don't find that there's much earnest grappling with ideas about the meaning of life.'

'There's another wonderful section where Birek, the young dissident, has lunch with a literary agent, and by mistake crosses all the unwritten barriers of literary conversation. At the end of it all, he says to his friend, in a very puzzled way, that in Czecho-slovakia, it was dangerous to criticise the government, but here it seems to be dangerous not to criticise the government . . .'

'Well, I do think we are very complacent about the freedom we have in this country, and obviously we do have a sort of freedom they don't have on the other side of the Iron Curtain. But there is a kind of intolerance amongst liberal, leftist intellectuals in this country, and I find that rather shocking. There's an intolerance, so that when someone says they think Mrs Thatcher is wonderful, they do become complete pariahs in certain circles, and vice versa. There are some little issues, which are touchstones, like Nicaragua or South Africa or whatever. There's a sort of Orwellian intolerance, in certain liberal circles, which isn't speci-fically political intolerance, but is quite dangerous and dis-agreeable.'

In at least two other novels as well, Read has looked at Britain through the eyes of foreigners.

'Yes, on the one hand, it's a convenient way of looking afresh at your own society. It's also partly because I felt, particularly grow-ing up in North Yorkshire, something of a foreigner in that society. That's partly because my father, as I said before, no longer belonged to the farming stock he came from, partly because my mother was foreign (she came from German extraction and was brought up in Scotland) and felt very alienated by British upper-class society. Partly, it's to do with being a Catholic.'

The novelist Antonia White once remarked that Catholicism was not so much a religion, as a nationality.

'Obviously, if you're one of those old upper-class English

Catholics, you've found your niche in British society, you feel very comfortable in it. But if you're not one of those Catholics, if you are Catholic purely by faith, by conviction, you do feel to some extent alienated, first of all from a country that has a Protestant tradition, and a Protestant constitution, and also from the sort of rationalist, sceptical, intellectual atmosphere in this country at the moment. You are an oddity if you really insist upon Christian beliefs in certain circles in this country.'

Muffled noises above indicated that his younger children, a boy aged ten and a little girl of seven, had arrived home from school. Ten minutes later, they would be creeping down shyly, in their maroon and grey school uniforms, asking us if they might watch the television in the sitting room, while the engineer wound up his cables. At this point, their father looked a shade anxious that the sounds might appear on the recording, but relieved that his ordeal might soon be at an end. He does not enjoy the fame of being a novelist.

'I think fame is an appalling thing, and I've seen it spoil the lives of not just some of my contemporaries, but a lot of my father's. Several of my father's friends became very famous – Henry Moore, and T. S. Eliot, and people like that. I think it makes life impossible. You get surrounded by parasitic people who want to befriend you because you are famous, and it becomes very difficult to know who your true friends are.'

Writers, he says, are pulled in two directions. They know that if they are not to some extent famous, they cannot make a living out of their writing. So they have to promote themselves, or allow themselves to be promoted, as interesting people:

'But on the other hand, one has a longing for anonymity, not just out of a sense of humility, but because anonymity is really rather essential to the collecting of material that will then go into the novels.

'No,' he added, quietly, 'I think fame is a nightmare.'

— • —

# IRIS MURDOCH

— • —

DBE 1987; CBE 1976; fellow of St Anne's College, Oxford, since 1948, Hon. Fellow, 1963; born Dublin 15 July 1919; married 1956, John Oliver Bayley. Education: Froebel Educational Insitute; Badminton School, Bristol; Somerville College, Oxford (Lit. Hum. 1st class 1942), Hon. Fellow, 1977. Asst Principal Treasury 1942–4; Administrative Officer with UNRRA, working in London, Belgium and Austria, 1944–6; Sarah Smithson studentship in philosophy, Newnham College, Cambridge, 1947–8; Lecturer, RCA 1963–7. Member of Irish Academy, 1970; Hon. Member: American Academy of Arts and Letters, 1982. Hon. Fellow of Newnham College, Cambridge, 1986. **Novels**: *Sartre, Romantic Rationalist*, 1953; *Under the Net*, 1954; *The Flight from the Enchanter*, 1955; *The Sandcastle*, 1957; *The Bell*, 1958; *A Severed Head*, 1961 (play, Criterion, 1963); *An Unofficial Rose*, 1962; *The Unicorn*, 1963; *The Italian Girl*, 1964 (play, Criterion, 1967); *The Red and the Green*, 1965; *The Time of the Angels*, 1966; *The Nice and the Good*, 1968; *Bruno's Dream*, 1969; *A Fairly Honourable Defeat*, 1970; *The Sovereignty of Good*, 1970; *An Accidental Man*, 1971; *The Black Prince*, 1973 (James Tait Black Memorial Prize); *The Sacred and Profane Love Machine*, 1974 (Whitbread Prize); *A Word Child*, 1975; *Henry and Cato*, 1976; *The Fire and the Sun*, 1977; *The Sea, the Sea*, 1978 (Booker Prize, 1978); *Nuns and Soldiers*, 1980; *The Philosopher's Pupil*, 1983; *The Good Apprentice*, 1985; *Acastos*, 1986; *The Book and the Brotherhood*, 1988. **Plays**: *The Servants and the Snow* (Greenwich) 1970; *The Three Arrows* (Arts, Cambridge), 1972; *Art and Eros* (National Theatre), 1980. **Poetry**: *A Year of Birds*, 1978.

# FLIGHT TO
# THE ENCHANTRESS

— • —

'John Mortimer, did you say?' said Iris Murdoch, as I listed her fellow contributors to the radio series and to this book. 'Who is that?' She turned away from the window, the autumnal morning light shining through the dancing specks of dust, and illuminating her small, round, but imposing figure in all its considerable majesty. I mentioned various Mortimer novels like *Paradise Postponed* and the Rumpole books and their television series. 'Oh, yes', she said, remembering hearing him on the radio. She does not have a television.

For some reason, I had imagined she would live in a spacious flat on the upper floor of a large, early nineteenth-century house built of warm sandstone. But our car had turned left into a quiet, not very fashionable, area in North Oxford. Her modest brick house is among the largest in a street of small detached and semi-detached houses in 1920s or 1930s style, each with a tiny front garden, separated from the road by a low wall or a beech or privet hedge or a poplar tree or two. There are some net curtains. It looks very ordinary. Iris Murdoch was once asked if the ordinary bored her. 'No', she replied, 'the ordinary is extraordinary.' She opened the ordinary door, and smiled her enchanting, extraordinary smile.

She was wearing a black velvet jacket, a blue blouse, a navy cotton skirt with a flowered pattern, navy blue stockings and flat black espadrilles. Usually, Iris Murdoch guards her privacy from interviewers carefully. But she welcomed us warmly. The BBC engineer, she said, had already arrived. He was surrounded with wires.

Inside, books are ready to devour the house. Even in the downstairs lavatory, Greek volumes line the walls. Only in the kitchen, it seems, do other things hold sway. A tub of washing, and a pile of dirty crockery await her. By the living-room door stands a sociable tray of drink bottles. Publishers' catalogues and letters lie about the room, with records by Mahler and Mozart. She shares the house (and also a London flat) with her husband John Bayley, Warton Professor of English Literature, to whom she has been happily married for over thirty years. Soon, we are happily settled in comfortable armchairs. In response to her questions, I am launching into stage two of my life history, when the engineer is ready to start recording. We switch to *her* life history and begin at the beginning.

She was an only child. Her father worked as a civil servant; her mother, like Anthony Burgess's mother, was a singer, so there was always music at home. She looked to me like someone who had always had the security of being loved. I wondered, cheerfully, whether she had been dreadfully spoilt as a child?

'Certainly not, no', she said decisively, her back straight. 'Well, perhaps I was spoilt . . . My relations with my parents were so harmonious and we were so anxious to please each other and make each other happy, that I don't think the question really arose. I had a very harmonious childhood.'

Her parents moved to London when she was one, but she was born in Dublin. Does she feel very Irish?

'Yes, I am completely Irish.'

'And what does that mean to you?'

'Well, it means worrying about Ireland, and feeling very deeply moved and upset by things that happen in Ireland.'

Both her parents were Irish Protestants – her father's religious background was Quaker evangelical, her mother's Anglican. 'My parents weren't particularly devout, they weren't regular churchgoers, but they both had deep religious feelings. My mother taught me to pray as soon as I could speak, and I was given to feel very early on a sense of a religious dimension to the world – of, as it were, an elsewhere, which was religion.'

But, like most adolescents brought up inside a religious faith, she became uneasy about it at a certain age. At eighteen, partly due to the influence of her left-wing, progressive school, Badminton, she gave up religion for Marxism: 'Indira Gandhi was there when I was there, and a lot of left-wing people and German Jewish refugee girls, so we were very politically conscious.'

During the war, Iris Murdoch left Oxford University, where she'd been studying classics, and was conscripted into the civil service. She later worked for the UN, helping refugees in Belgium and Austria. Eventually, she was able to return to Oxford to pick up her studies and to teach philosophy.

She still retains many of her old feelings about social justice, and voted Labour until quite recently. But some of her views about socialism have changed, and she is currently voting Conservative.

'I couldn't accept the Labour party's doctrine on defence, or their reluctance about belonging to Europe – I feel strongly that we must make ourselves into Europeans – I don't like the line many of them take on Ireland, and I think that Margaret Thatcher's government has done a number of good things. There are a number of good things it has failed to do, but I think it's done some good.'

Iris Murdoch's first novel, *Under the Net*, was published in 1954, when she was 34. She considers it now as an oddity, 'a sort of freak – full of a *joie de vivre* of a rather childish kind.' Among her earlier books, the one she likes best is *The Bell*, the novel about a lay community camped outside the abbey home of an enclosed order of nuns. She says it's a much more composed and thoughtful, sturdier and better constructed book than the earlier ones.

The theme of *The Bell* is human frailty and the conflict of good and evil. Why has the search for goodness in fallen world come to absorb her so much? One answer is the immense influence of Plato on her life.

'Plato is king. Plato established the notion that human life is about the battle between good and evil. A. N. Whitehead said that all Western philosophy is footnotes to Plato. He set up the first great philosophical picture of the human soul and of this mysterious business we're all involved in, and when I really started studying all Plato's dialogues, I was absolutely enchanted and taken over by this extraordinary mind.'

Plato broke away from the pre-Socratic philosophers who thought in terms of a general rhythm or harmony of nature, rather like Taoists. Such thinkers esteem harmony rather than virtue. A modern example of this sort of thinking is the twentieth-century psychologist, Carl Jung. She says Jung is a magician; that he wants people to come to terms with the dark side of their soul and to recognise the great archetypal images and to harmonise themselves into some sort of serene unification of the soul.

'That's the opposite of what I think. If one's looking for philosophical pictures, I would follow one which makes it very clear that human beings live on a line between good and evil, and every moment of one's life is involved in movement upon this line, in one's thoughts, as well as in the things one does.'

In 1970, Iris Murdoch published a novel which focused specially sharply on the destructive power of the wrong side of the line. It was titled *A Fairly Honourable Defeat* – the fairly honourable defeat, that is, of good by evil. It centres on the very happy, apparently stable marriage of Rupert and Hilda. To begin with, their only troubles seem to be their drop-out son, and Hilda's unstable sister, Morgan, who has just returned from America. Then Morgan's ex-lover, Julius King, enters in the role of Mephistopheles, and decides to give the whole cosy arrangement a severe jolt.

'The book is a sort of allegory . . . Tallis, Morgan's husband, is supposed to be a broken-down sort of good man, or one might say, to use an oriental term, he's a kind of high incarnation of the good spirit. His conflict with Julius is the central part of the book. Julius represents the dark angel, the prince of this world, and ultimately, of course, Tallis and Julius recognise each other because they are both spiritual beings.'

Writing about good people is difficult for novelists, because they may often be nearly invisible, not needing to make great waves of self-assertion. The dark angels may grip the reader's imagination more strongly. In several novels, Iris Murdoch explores figures like Julius, ranging around with an extraordinary, deadly, wasting, dangerous power like jokers or wild cards. The character Pin, in *The Sacred and Profane Love Machine*, has some of those qualities. Does she actually know such people?

'Well, I've known very powerful people. In all sorts of ways, people often find themselves under a spell – whether it's through their work, or through religion or through falling in love and so on. . . . One might say that magic is the enemy of religion, that religion degenerates into magic. . . . But persistent religions do have magical elements, and it's a short step from loving God, or wanting to save one's soul, to wanting power. You feel you are going to transcend the ordinary human state, and be in some higher state. And there are people who achieve, or at any rate, exude, this kind of aura of magical power. I mean ordinary people, people who are teachers or artists . . . many, many kinds of people in ordinary situations. And other people want this. It is a very familiar human situation that people are fascinated by a magician, a man who seems to be either very good (it sometimes takes this form), or (more often) simply very powerful and frightening.'

In *A Fairly Honourable Defeat*, Julius emerges as particularly frightening and powerful. He is able to set up the trap for each person so perfectly because he judges their weaknesses correctly – that Morgan wants to eat all her cakes and have them too, that Rupert is fond of holding forth about goodness in a self-satisfied sort of way, and so on. At the end of the book, he askes Tallis whether he concedes that he is an instrument of justice. Tallis just smiles. Does the author concede that Julius is an instrument of justice?

'Well, no, because what he sees is only part of the picture. Besides, it's not for him to go round punishing people, so he's not a proper instrument of justice.'

'So it's justice without mercy?'

'Yes.'

'I suppose if Christianity is about anything it's about justice with mercy?'

'I think the concept of justice is a very difficult one unless you use it in a secular context – relating to courts of law and how they operate, and what you blame people for. Ideas of justice alter, and people used to be blamed for things they are now not blamed for. This would be a tempering of justice with intelligent understanding. But if you think of justice belonging to a personal God, then this is a much more difficult question. I think there can be perverted ideas of justice involved in a religion. If one thinks of all the pictures in churches of the Last Judgment, with people going up to heaven and other people being trampled on and cast down, this is a very grim idea of justice. I personally don't believe in a personal god, and I don't believe in the Last Judgment or anything of the sort.'

'I suppose it could be said that many Christians understand justice as the recognition of truth?'

'I think the concept to hang on to is truth. Let justice look after itself. Justice suggests judging other people, and punishment and so on. Truth and love are much more fundamental concepts and these are the matters we are primarily dealing with.'

Outside, beyond the French window, wind shakes the apple tree in the tiny garden. A windfall bounces to the leaf-strewn grass. The sunshine flickers round the room.

'Why is stealing wrong?' That is the simple moral question Hilda's shop-lifting, but intelligent, drop-out son asks of Tallis. Tallis, taken by surprise, replies unconvincingly. Others fail the question too. Why is stealing wrong?

'That's a good question. One good reason is that if you steal, you get into trouble, you may ruin your life, you may make your parents very unhappy and so on. But I think, basically, stealing is a kind of lying, you're not in the open, you're not in the clear, you're not being truthful if you're a thief, and stealing usually damages a lot of people. It will damage the person from whom you steal. Of course, some shoplifters will say, "Well, I only steal from Marks and Spencers, that's all right. They can afford it", and so on. But it's a very bad kind of thing to do, because it is a kind of lie, and if your life rests upon a lot of lies of this sort, then it's a very bad sort of life.'

'In the novel, there's the constant idea that lying ruins relation-ship . . .'

'Yes.'

'Do you ever tell lies now?'

'Well, I sometimes tell social lies, but I think I would not be too stern upon that . . . One very often says something which is not quite what one thinks in order not to hurt people. Kant thought you should never ever tell a lie. Even if somebody comes to murder someone else and says, "Where is he?", he thought you should appeal to the nobler aspect of the would-be murderer and tell him the truth in the hope he'd change his mind! Well, I think most of us would not be quite as strict as that.'

Unlike novelists like Brian Moore, who write to discover what happens to their characters, Iris Murdoch writes nothing until she knows how the story will develop:

'I plan it in enormous detail down to the last conversation before I write the first sentence. So it takes a long time to invent it.'

'Is it true that you write your novels in longhand?'

'Yes, yes. How else can one write a novel?' she asked mischievously.

'Some people use computers . . .'

'I alter things all the time as I go along. I can't type, and – *a fortiori* – I don't have anything to do with word processors. I would have thought it extraordinarily awkward to alter what one is writing if one's got a machine between you and the page. I think this particular closeness makes it easier for one to work very finely and to keep on altering things, improving them, polishing them.'

'Do you allow people to edit your books?'

She looked startled. 'Well, no . . . but I don't think anyone has ever tried to.' I wasn't a bit surprised. We both laughed. 'I think that with one of my very, very early novels, someone suggested that I should leave a character out. But I refused to do so.' Her back straightened. She chuckled. 'Quite rightly. My publishers are very kind and nice.' I had the distinct impression she would change publishers if they altered a word.

'Do you ever stop being a novelist? I mean, when you write to your bank manager, do you write an ordinary straightforward business letter?'

'You mean, do I produce rather a flowery letter to my bank manager?' We both laughed again. 'No,' I said, 'I mean an imaginative, creative letter . . .'

'Well, one likes to write a clear and elegant letter. I like writing letters and I write a lot of letters. I think there are different styles for different relationships.' Quite so. No more information there.

An inspired portrait of Dame Iris hangs in the National Portrait Gallery, off Trafalgar Square. In the background of the portrait is a picture by Titian, called *The Flaying of Marsyas*. Marsyas claimed he was as good a musician as Apollo. When he lost the competition, he was flayed by the god. In the picture, Apollo is kneeling and very lovingly removing the skin. For Iris Murdoch, the picture is a profound image of the death of the self. Marsyas with the help of the god is losing his egoism in an agony, which is also an ecstasy. For Iris Murdoch, religion is about the death of the ego, about the stripping away of illusions to reveal truth. Little wonder that she is uncomfortable with television, a medium in which those involved work in a totally unnatural environment in order to create an illusion of naturalness.

A year or so ago, in one of her rare forays into the world of television, Dame Iris was interviewed about her work by an Icelandic television company. The interviewer evidently found the characters in her novels extraordinary. Did the ordinary bore her, she asked? No, she replied, the ordinary is extraordinary. I asked her to expand.

'The more you get to known about ordinary people, the more startled you are. Most people have a dignified facade, and you have to know them very well to discover what's going on in their minds, what frightens them, what's been happening to them, and so on. These things, of course, one conceals in the interests of civilised life and in order to protect one's own mode of being. I don't think one has any duty to exhibit oneself, as it were, to people except when you know them well. Or to expect that other people will tell you all about themselves. Why should they? But I think that people are terribly strange and terribly different from one another. I have known people who are much odder than the people in my books.'

'Some of your characters are rather like characters in myths, aren't they?'

But Dame Iris was cautious about myths, though she admits her head is full of them. The danger for a writer of a traditional novel, she maintains, is of the myth taking over the character, who instead should be full of surprises. She sees the main weakness of her own novels as her failure to animate her characters as much as great novelists do:

'Great writers like Dostoyevsky, Proust or Dickens or Tolstoy, can animate every character so that they can be quite peculiar and full of surprises. A lift boy or another minor figure can suddenly be quite startling.'

'Even in the most tragic situations, you make time to make fun of your characters. Do you enjoy that?'

'Oh, I think a novel, however sad it is, is essentially comic. Everybody can be made fun of, innumerable comic situations arise all the time in ordinary life.'

She sees humour as also making space in novels to carry something very, very sad. 'Shakespeare is full of terribly sad humour. When there's something very touching and pathetic that's happening, that's also very funny. This also makes space for tragic things to be extended and understood.'

In a number of her books – for instance, *The Sea, the Sea*, *The Good Apprentice* and *Nuns and Soldiers*, water seems to be used as a symbol of cleansing. She said she did this instinctively, rather than consciously. She loves the sea and swimming. Water is a deep symbol – frightening, and murderous, and also cleansing and forgiving. But she thinks there is a danger in symbolism. 'I think a writer of a traditional novel is wise to rub out or fudge over a piece of symbolism that is coming out too clearly.'

Writing such books, and keeping up such a high output, seemed to me to be potentially exhausting, both mentally and emotionally. She's absorbed in a novel almost continuously, and sometimes writes philosophy as well as fiction. She relaxes by listening to the radio or to music, reading and sewing. She also likes conversation very much, but doesn't get as much as she would like, because she works all day.

She loves singing, and was once trained by a singing teacher. At home during her childhood, her mother would play the piano. 'We would sing all those marvellous popular songs of the 1930s, which are great songs compared with what's called a popular song nowadays. And lots of other songs, folk songs and opera. But when does one get a chance to sing now, unless one belongs to a choir? If one starts singing when you're with friends, they begin to look a bit shifty – ' she laughed ' – and think they'd rather you stopped – however charming one's voice may be, which in my case is getting rather rusty. People who don't like singing resent it very much.'

Sometimes people say of Iris Murdoch's work that it is obsessed with the moral and spiritual problems of the same group of middle-class intellectuals appearing in different guises in different books, and that they would be all much less anxious and better adjusted if they had to do a decent day's work in the rough-and-tumble of the world outside university cities. I threw this into the hat.

'Good heavens, people work very hard in university cities. The notion that there isn't any serious work which belongs to intellectual people is a very dangerous and misleading idea. People work extremely hard, as people in the civil service work hard. When I was a civil servant, I was filled with the greatest respect for the people I knew there, who were not only very clever, but extremely hardworking, extremely conscientious. Few of my characters don't work. They are teachers or writers or painters or civil servants. Some of them are servants. So the notion that they are all idlers, just sitting round examining their conscience, is not just.'

'But they tend to be middle-class intellectuals with a certain standard of living?'

'Well, not all of them. But I don't think this is important. One has got to write about what one knows. If I knew a lot about coal mining, I would write about coal mining. If I knew what it was like to be a sailor, I'd write about sailors. I very much wish I did know about other things. An aspiring novelist should take note – the more you know about anything is a help to you in writing a novel. I don't know about physics and chemistry for example. I wish I did. But there it is, one's life has certain limitations.'

Time and again, Iris Murdoch's books explore Christian themes, the search for goodness in a fallen world, selfishness versus unselfishness, powerlessness versus power and so on. But it is always, or nearly always, the search for goodness without God. Why does she, in her characters, reject God?

'Not all my characters reject God. But I can't accept the idea of a personal God of the Judaeo-Christian kind. A God who is pictured as living somewhere else, as being somewhere else, as being a judge, to whom, after surviving death, I may or may not come. I can't accept this mythology as anything literal. I think these things are symbolic.' She paused. 'I even think that the idea of a personal God is a hindrance to religion.'

The second commandment, she says, supports this:

'Thou shalt not make thee any graven image, or any likeness of any thing that is in heaven above, or that is in the earth beneath, or that is in the water beneath the earth:

'Thou shalt not bow down thyself unto them, nor serve them: for I the Lord thy God am a jealous God.'

She says that the idea that religion goes beyond imagery and idols is a form of Platonism. Plato pictures human life as a progress from one image to another, a pilgrimage through the destruction of images, and the discovery of a spiritual truth or higher form of being which lies beyond. Here she feels close to Buddhism.

At one stage in her life, Iris Murdoch thought she might become a Buddhist. She regards the situation of Jesus and Buddha as similar in that they are both men who lived on earth and lived very significant lives and are both mystical figures. But she thinks of herself as really a Christian, because it is the mystical Christ she feels close to, and she has known Jesus all her life.

'I haven't any feelings about God the Father, but I have very strong feelings about Christ.'

'But you don't think Christ is God?'

'No, I don't believe in the divinity of Christ. I believe Saint Paul was, in a way, in this situation. What he believed in was the risen Christ, that is the Christ that would work in people's lives, and change their lives.'

'You say you don't believe in God, the divinity of Christ, the afterlife, yet you still think of yourself as a Christian. How can you possibly do that with so many reservations?'

'Well, this is my own view of the matter. I think of myself as a Christian and I don't see why I shouldn't. I think there is a movement in theology in this direction. It is "demythologisation", which is very important now in Christian thinking, and that's why I'm sorry the present Pope discourages this sort of speculation.' She want on:

'I think it would be terrible if religion were to disappear from the lives of people, and it does disappear from the lives of young people very often. I am surprised to find how many young people don't even know the Christian stories, let alone having any conception of a religion of any sort.'

What Dame Iris would like to see is a more Buddhist attitude to religion. 'That is, not insisting on certain literal beliefs, but insisting on a religious mode of being involved in prayer, meditation, and relating yourself to spiritual images which are vessels of grace to you, as the image of Christ is. I think there is a real danger that the west will become de-Christianised and that we shall lose Christianity if we don't think of it in a wider and deeper way: trying to understand religion as to do with holiness and a reverence for what is holy and good, and feeling that the soul is a spiritual place, even if it won't survive one's body.'

Again, the background for this is Plato: the idea that the soul has many parts and many compartments, and many forms of being, and that religion is about the purification of the soul and the enlargement of the soul. Art, she believes, can have a religious function, along with religion and religious imagery, in re-affirming the sense of another dimension, another place.

'If one reads nineteenth-century novels, people are always praying. Nowadays, I think people very often don't pray. They think that prayer is a superstitious attempt to gain favour and so on. But the idea of prayer and the idea of meditation as it appears in Buddhism and Hinduism, is very important – that you withdraw yourself from your ordinary persona and are quiet. This is why I like the Quaker idea of silence – that you remove yourself into a kind of silence where you realise that the things bothering you are very largely unimportant, that your anxieties are unworthy.'

'Do you pray?'

'Well, I meditate. Yes, I think I pray, but then the distinction between prayer and meditation becomes rather unclear.'

'Would you like to be able to go to church and take communion with other Christians?'

'I could if I chose to, I suppose. Nobody would stop me. I don't know. I am afraid that I am put off by – which is very foolish – I am put off by the modern rituals and I do hanker for the old Prayer Book and for the words which are so wonderful and so solemn. Yes, I would like to in a way, but it is not something I feel any urge to do.'

Iris Murdoch has now published twenty-three novels. Dickens published fifteen. What keeps her writing? Is it because she wants Christian ideas to work without God, and they just don't?

'No, I don't think so. I write because I like it, this is my art form and I want to write better, and I want to create works of art. It's very dangerous to write as a pedagogue. I think good novelists, for instance Sartre, are damaged by a desire to put across a philosophical creed. You have to follow your instinct as an artist, I think, and not try to be a teacher in art.'

'What do you think you would need so that you wouldn't need to write any more?'

'I can't imagine not needing to write. I should be very unhappy if I couldn't write.'

— • —

# A. N. WILSON

— • —

FRSL; born 27 October, 1950; married 1971, Katherine Duncan-Jones; two daughters. Education: Rugby, New College, Oxford (MA). Chancellor's Essay Prize, 1971, and Ellerton Theological Prize, 1975. FRSL, 1981. **Novels**: *The Sweets of Pimlico*, 1977 (John Llewellyn Rhys Memorial Prize, 1978); *Unguarded Hours*, 1978; *Kindly Light*, 1979; *The Healing Art*, 1980 (Somerset Maugham Award, 1981; Arts Council National Book Award, 1981; Southern Arts Prize, 1981); *Who Was Oswald Fish?*, 1981; *Wise Virgin*, 1982 (W.H. Smith Literary Award, 1983); *Scandal*, 1983; *Gentlemen in England*, 1985; *Love Unknown*, 1986. **Non-fiction**: *The Laird of Abbotsford*, 1980 (John Llewellyn Rhys Memorial Prize, 1981); *A Life of John Milton*, 1983; *Hilaire Belloc*, 1984; *How Can We Know?*, 1985; (jointly) *The Church in Crisis*, 1986; *Tolstoy*, 1988. Numerous reviews and literary articles.

# SERMONS ON THE MOUNT

— • —

I interviewed A. N. Wilson in bed. It made a change from studios
or front rooms. We had begun in more normal circumstances, in
the Victorian-style drawing room of his tall four-floored aesthete's
house in a quiet tree-lined street towards the centre of Oxford. On
the walls of the narrow, pleasantly cluttered, double room, oil
paintings of nineteenth-century religious ecstasy and various
prints and etchings obscured the William-Morris-style wallpaper.
Battered books were piled on tables. A loose unfitted carpet
covered the floorboards. The only modern piece of furniture was
a small television set. In neighbouring streets, overshadowed by
high college walls, junk shops recycle second-hand bookcases and
other furniture for yet another generation of students. He and his
wife (an academic, older than himself), have lived in the house for
sixteen years. They have two teenage daughters.

The radio recording, which I opened by mentioning his
family, had not begun well. His father had been managing director
of a Stoke-on-Trent pottery, who retired early to a Welsh village,
when Wilson was ten. Andrew Wilson was the youngest of three
children, and so a quasi-only child. I had just asked him about his
childhood and family, and he had said he didn't much want to talk
about them, and yes, he loved the Welsh, but no, he didn't feel the
least Welsh, when a loud knocking from the neighbouring back
garden relieved us both by sending the engineer's sound-level
needle surging towards the red.

A discreet peer round the window curtains revealed the neighbour just beginning to hammer together with gusto a wooden
garden shed. I wondered whether we might explain the problem to

him, but Andrew Wilson looked very shy and said he would be embarrassed to tell him what he was doing.

The solution was to lug half the sound equipment upstairs to the small first-floor front bedroom. I sat on a wooden armchair. He lay on the duvet on the high bed, in a woolly patterned sweater and cord trousers, propped up on pillows, surrounded by an alarm clock, piles of clean socks and a telephone, his hands neatly folded on his stomach and a seraphic smile on his face. Before me was the solemn young man of letters, with the junior guards officer exterior, biographer of Sir Walter Scott, Milton and Tolstoy, winner of various literary prizes, former supporter of the Conservative Party, newly announced convert to Labour, critic and devotee of the Church of England, once a scourge among reviewers, now grinning like a twelve-year-old.

The levee was about to begin.

Andrew Wilson's writing career began at an early age: at six, he composed some short stories; at fourteen, he wrote his first novel, then burnt it two years later.

About that time, Wilson first became aware of the life and work of Leo Tolstoy, the great Russian novelist, whose writings, spiritual search, and rejection of the trappings of wealth in his later years have since haunted Wilson's life. 1988 saw the publication of Wilson's 570-page biography of Tolstoy. His initial discovery of Tolstoy was a bit like a conversion experience. He was a teenager at Rugby at the time.

'I've never had a conversion experience in the religious sense of the word, but it was . . . it was very powerful. I felt overwhelmed by the figure of Tolstoy and his ideas – by their simplicity, by the idea that we all know within ourselves how to live really.'

He thinks he had already read some of Tolstoy's shorter stories by then – like *The Cossacks*, and dipped into *War and Peace*.

'But then a very remarkable man called R. V. Sampson, whom I've never met since, came and gave us one of those talks that kind people give to school children when they've nothing better to do with their time; and he told us all about Tolstoy, the man, whom I found absolutely fascinating – the story of this complex, and in many ways, self-contradictory, passionate genius, deciding in middle life that the most important thing in the world wasn't to write a great novel (he'd already done that), wasn't to be a literary

genius, but was to discover how to live in this world, on this
earth . . .'

His blue eyes looked into the far distance.

'We all know', he said slowly, 'that it's wrong to pursue money
for its own sake; we all know it's wrong to pursue power for its
own sake; and that the death of self is the beginning of wisdom.
I suppose – roughly speaking – that's what Tolstoy drew out of
the gospels, with a certain amount of Buddhism and other
religions.'

Pacifism, too, meant a lot to Tolstoy; and vegetarianism,
which also meant a lot to the young Wilson. He gave up eating
anything except nut cutlets, and worried terribly whether his
shoes were leather.

By the age of sixteen, he had already been an enthusiastic
convert to various beliefs, ranging from a simple sort of evangelical
Christianity, to atheism, to Marxism, with special devotion to the
teachings of Chairman Mao. But at seventeen or eighteen, he
decided to become a Roman Catholic. He said he could tell me
about it only as he might tell me about the behaviour of a total
stranger:

'I can't remember any of the sensations or inner belief which
led me to do it. It now strikes me as the most fantastic possible fact
about myself.'

It began, it seems, with reading the work of the famous
nineteenth-century convert to Rome, Cardinal Newman.

'He was the most wonderful and seductive stylist. His *Apologia*, particularly, but also his sermons, began like a strange
romantic music in my head. But I was also haunted by the argument of the *Apologia*, which, very roughly speaking, is:

'If Christ founded a church (in other words, if God came to
earth as a man and started a divine society), where is it today? And,
if you count backwards – if you start off nowadays, and work your
way back through history – and let's say, you're an Anglican, you
eventually reach the disturbing figure of Henry the Eighth; or if
you're a Methodist, you reach the much less disturbing figure of
John Wesley, starting out this particular religious group. If, on the
other hand, you are a Roman Catholic, you can – particularly if
you read the right books – follow the argument all the way back, so
that the founder of the Roman Catholic church is Our Lord
Himself.

'That was the absolutely clinching argument, as far as I was concerned.'

'Why do you find it unbelievable now that you found that persuasive at the time?'

'I find it absolutely extraordinary that anybody can read the New Testament, and let's say, the parables of Christ in St Luke's gospel, and imagine, let us say, the Good Samaritan taking off that poor man to the inn, and leaving his two pence, and saying, "Oh, and by the way, it is terribly important that you should belong to a particular religious denomination"; or the Prodigal Son, rushing into his father's arms, and learning, "and oh, by the way, it is tremendously important that you should have views about bishops, priests and deacons", or whatever it might be.'

'That strikes me', he went on, 'as utterly fantastical. The whole process of ecclesiastical history, interesting as I once found it, seems almost detached in my mind from really important religious issues – if you like, from the everlasting gospel.'

I said that he certainly seems to have changed a great deal from the days he was a Roman Catholic. He was once quoted as saying that the present Pope is one of the bossiest, most narrow-minded men ever to sit of St Peter's throne.

'I wouldn't wish to repeat that', he said. 'I think it might be rather offensive to people. But', he added, without a pause, 'I think it is probably true all the same.'

He made amends:

'I love the present Pope, I like bossy, biffing self-confident people. And I know that if I had been a pupil of his at Cracow University, when he was a teacher, I would have a tremendous affection for the Pope. But he ought to go and live as a parish priest in Manhattan or somewhere, and discover what it is like to live in a world where issues are slightly more complex than they are in his own head.'

It was in 1977, when he was twenty-seven, that Wilson's first novel *Sweets of Pimlico* was published. The following year, it won the John Llewellyn Rhys Memorial Prize. It was dedicated to Iris Murdoch, whom he admires enormously, not only as a writer, but as a person. Her husband was one of his former tutors. They live a mile or so away from the Wilsons, and meet fairly often.

After graduating from New College, Oxford, he had taught for a while at the university, and at a tutorial agency, and as a schoolmaster in Middlesex. In 1977, he returned to Oxford as a lecturer.

His next two novels – *Unguarded Hours* and *Kindly Light* shone a sharp satirical light on the Church of England. They describe with zest the adventures of one Norman Shotover, a sacked solicitor's clerk. One day, Shotover wakes from a drunken service to find himself ordained a priest by a self-employed bishop given to on-the-spot ordinations. He considers he should make an honest man of himself and enter theological college – only to find it a total disgrace. Shotover later gets involved in the CIA, the Catholic Institute of Alfonso.

He dashed each of these novels off, he says, in three weeks.

He is now rather ashamed of the Shotover novels in some ways – not for their content, but because he doesn't think they are as skilful as he once did.

'They were meant as entertainments. The fact that I no longer find them entertaining is largely because they just aren't quite as skilful, or as funny, or as deft as they might be.'

To what extent did the novels emerge from his direct experience of the church, of the one particular Anglo-Catholic theological college he briefly attended, of Oxford, of teaching?

'I can only say that, as far as I can remember (it is fifteen years ago), I had to play down real-life details I knew about real Anglican theological colleges. They are places of the purest lunacy. They were then, and I'm sure they are now.'

Wilson would have supposed that the way to learn how to be a priest was to go and watch a parish priest in action, 'not to lock yourself up with a lot of other religious eccentrics (usually in a place which is far from the kind of geographical area where you will be working) and fill your head with a lot of fairly esoteric concerns.'

'You know the sort of thing which interests theological students', he went on. 'If you are high church, it is what you wear in church. If you are low church, it is an emotional experience. But neither of these things are necessarily going to stand you in good stead, when it comes to dealing with someone who is dying of cancer, or teaching children the rudiments of the Christian religion, which is what parish priests have to do.'

'One of the things you sent up in the novel is the extreme campness of the theological college. Was it really that bad?'

'Well, I wouldn't necessarily say camp is bad. But yes, that is not my discovery. Everyone knows that about the high-church wing of the Church of England.'

'Do you yourself feel much less hostile to the Church of England now?'

'I love the Church of England. I love it in all its dottiness and absurdity. And the fact that you might have camp high-church vicars, or mad low-church vicars, doesn't in the least disturb me. I think there is a danger of reading those two novels in a rather moralistic way, rather in the spirit that you might read a newspaper account of some clergyman being had up by the police or something. So what? It is only a little bit of it, as far as I am concerned, and rather an endearing bit.'

Someone who did not take the same view was the late, lamented novelist Barbara Pym, who was one of the judges for a literary prize for which the novels were submitted:

'As you know, she was not only a very good novelist, but also a devout churchwoman. She refused two years running to contemplate giving a prize to these books, as I learnt afterwards, because of their irreverent attitude towards the Church of England. Quite right too, I think.'

'Do you?'

'Well, I mean, jolly good for her. I'm delighted she took that line. It distresses me to think that I might have hurt anybody by writing those books.'

In 1980, Andrew Wilson published another novel *The Healing Art*, which won not one, but three, literary prizes. Pamela, a cool, rather beautiful Oxford don in her thirties, is told she has cancer and has only a few months to live. She has a brief affair with an American girl, there are various medical muddles, and the novel explores the possibility of healing through prayer, and also through a loving marriage. At the end of the book, Wilson consigns two of the less likeable characters to flames – not exactly hell fire, but a fire at New College. Does he still like that novel? He had heard parts read aloud on *Woman's Hour*, some months before.

'I was very struck, listening to it, how good some bits were. But there are bits which I would certainly re-write now, if I were in charge . . . But I shall leave it as it stands. I think the melo-dramatic ending is rather absurd.'

But he still thinks the book is dealing with delicate and inter-esting subjects – whether the two women, who are told by the doctor they are dying, fundamentally put their trust in modern medicine, or whether they trust in deeper, less rational things.

One of the novel's characters puts the Christian view that any miraculous healing only bears significance if the person healed is able to feel the whole of life transformed: devoted to truth, not fantasy; to kindness, not malice; to serenity, not panic.

'Miracles are not just magic tricks. Some of the miracles in the Bible are obviously just magic tricks – like the rather silly things Moses is expected to do to prove to Pharaoh that his magic is better than the Egyptians' magic.'

He was referring, for instance, to the chapter in the Book of Exodus where Aaron's stick is turned into a snake:

'That', he went on, 'is only one step away from conjuring shows, isn't it? And, as far as one can see, doesn't have any spiritual significance. Whereas, when you read the story of the woman, who had had an issue of blood for years and years and years, touching the garment of Christ, and being healed, I would have said you are in touch with something infinitely more important.'

Pamela says she's happy to speak of God as if God existed, but that fundamentally deep down, she doesn't really imagine that God ever actually does anything. Her idea of God is 'of some clever old fellow at All Souls, someone who was supposed to be perfectly brilliant in their youth, but now prefers to be left alone in un-approachable light and not to be bothered with any request to repeat the tricks.' Does a part of A. N. Wilson see God in that way?

'That certainly is one false idea of God, which inevitably comes in and out of one's mind. Roughly speaking, it's what many of the eighteenth-century rationalists thought – they thought that God had fashioned the universe, and then left it to get on with its own rather mechanical life.'

He finds the idea of the universe being a purely mechanical or material place an extremely boring one, and one which does not actually correspond with experience.

'I suppose one of the people who explodes that idea most gloriously is William Blake – a great hero of mine. Remember that quatrain of Blake's:

'The atoms of Democritus
And Newton's particles of light
Are sands upon the Red Sea shore,
Where Israel's tents do shine so bright.'

'Just looking at the material universe and saying, "Well, that's all there is," or "God or the universe can only be what our finite, boring minds can make of it," is to rule out the whole possibility of imagination in life. And in fact, it's only through the exercise of the imagination that one glimpses who we might be, what the universe might be, and what might lie behind it, including that old gentleman in unapproachable light, about whom one always has the wrong ideas. We can't have the right ideas. All our ideas about God are false.'

A rhetorical overstatement? He insists he is coming to the conclusion that any idea about God that one tries to put into words is false.

'Blake called him "nobodaddy", the false god. The Bible has lots of words for false gods, and you could say the whole story of the Bible was people discovering false gods and eventually having to discard them.'

I remembered a school of Orthodox theology that tries to define God by defining what God is not. The principle is that God is so universal and so marvellous, that it is impossible to say what God is; but by clarifying what God is not, the theologians begin to understand.

'Yes, I'm very sympathetic to that school of thought. It's inevitable, if people have had private or collective religious or spiritual experiences that some of them want to put them into words – they want to form liturgies and they want to write hymns. I don't want to stop them doing that, so long as one doesn't stray into the rather idolatrous position of thinking that's the last word. There are no last words. If God means anything, which of course many people have questioned, it must mean something which is infinitely beyond our own wildest imaginings or dreams.'

I wondered in what way his own view of God had shifted over the last ten years, but he reckoned that to ask that question was to suggest he was a bit like Cardinal Newman, who wrote his *Apologia*, and was able to chronicle where he stood over the question of baptismal regeneration in 1833, and how it changed in 1835, and where he'd reached by 1840.

'It might be more sense to say, "Does my view of God shift from last Tuesday to next Thursday?" Sometimes I have the strongest sense of the reality of God, and at other times, it's totally absent, and in the times when it's totally absent, one naturally calls into question the definitions or the insights with which one has been so happy at other times.'

'How hard do you find it to relate those insights to your actual everyday life, and how you live it, and how you deal with people you meet?'

'Impossible to generalise, because it depends on what you mean by everyday life. There's a character in Ruth Draper's monologues (I love those things – she was a forerunner of Joyce Grenfell), who says, "Everyday life – that's what gets you in the end," which is certainly true.'

We both laughed. Somebody, he said, should have written a book in the Bible, which was not the Book of Job, confronting the great mysteries and losing everything, and watching ultimate evil confront God Himself.

'Somebody should have written a book about boring, everyday life – the sort of grind of routine, and shopping, and the car not working – then, does religion mean anything?'

It's the world so well depicted by Philip Larkin in his poems, or by Barbara Pym in her novels.

'It isn't so much that you doubt, it's a question of whether, let's say, Julian of Norwich – whose wonderful religious insights, on a good day, make you feel you're floating about the clouds – whether Julian of Norwich ever stood in the "eight-items-or-less" queue at the supermarket, watching a woman get out a chequebook and buy twenty-five items. Do you know what I mean?'

I knew just what he meant. 'Did she ever have to review other people's novels?' I added. He laughed some more.

'It's the sheer trivialisation of existence in the modern world, which to me drives out not merely religion, but all perception of the good and the beautiful and casts a kind of grey fog over life.'

Earlier, the man with me had said that kindness, not malice, was part of healing. Yet, in his past work, another personality called A. N. Wilson was not exactly a kind reviewer of other people's books. It was once said of him that he was reviled as the 'literary world's rapist'. Was it mischief, malice, insensitivity, malevolence, honesty? He now says he regrets the tone of some of those reviews.

'I don't quite know what got into me, but I do find that the causing of needless pain in the world, which is full of pain anyway, is unpardonable; and if you read a book which you know to be bad – and after all most books have their faults – there's no particular reason to say so.'

He now finds it hard to recepture his state of mind then:

'But I used to feel, "Here is someone expecting me to pay £10 for a book. This book is no good. Why shouldn't I say so?" I would rebut the idea that it was done in a spirit of complete malice. I think it was done in the spirit where I was heedless of the feelings of the author. It is possible to convey to the reader that you don't think much of the book, without getting out the sledgehammer. And also, it's possible not to review books at all, which I don't anymore.'

For a couple of years, A. N. Wilson was the literary editor of *The Spectator*. He eventually got sacked for cutting out a passage in an article, so turning a flattering reference to the television personality and author, Clive James, into a deadly insult. He did it for a joke one night when he was bored at the printers. While the job lasted, numerous novels crossed his desk. What impression did he get then of the state of fiction writing in England?

'Very little, because I've read almost none of them at the moment. I find it's a great distraction if you write novels, to read a lot of fiction, particularly contemporary fiction; and there are so many other things I want to read . . . I dare say that one of my thousand-and-one faults as a literary journalist was not being terribly interested in modern fiction.'

When writing himself, he always works out the plot before he starts, and knows who all the characters are.

'I sometimes even do a quick draft – say, of 10 000 words. But my usual way is just to make quite a lot of notes and then to draw a skeleton of the novel as I imagine it evolving. Usually, by the time I've written about a third of the novel, I find that I have got the skeleton slightly wrong and have to rewrite and rejig.'

'And do you write by longhand, like Iris Murdoch?'

'Yes. I've sometimes made the disastrous mistake of typing the first draft of the novel. I type the second draft of the novel.'

One reason why he says it is a mistake in his case is that he types very, very fast – inaccurately, but fast.

'I can do seven thousand words a day. And that's far too much if you are writing a novel. You need to mull over the prose, for one thing, and also, particularly in dialogue, you need to mull over whether it's really plausible that X could say this to Y, and whether it relates to what you want to happen in the next chapter, and what happened in the last chapter.'

He finds writing novels infinitely more absorbing than he used to.

'I'm now totally obsessed by my own novels, whereas in the past, I had a teaching job for most of the year, and I used to write my novels in the summer.'

In the winter months, he did not really think about the summer novel, and would not have worried very much if it had not come.

'Now I think about my novels day and night, the ones I'm writing. And I'm much more worried about getting it right, and much more worried about the whole texture of them, and the quality of the prose, and all those things. It appals me to think of the way I dashed off my early books.'

Does he want it to obsess him in that way?

'Well, I tell myself it would be marvellous when it all stops, and if the idea for the next novel didn't come, I wouldn't call it "writer's block", I would just say, "That's all, folks," and be completely delighted to do something else with my life. But I suspect, in fact, it would be shattering, because I suspect that for me, it's become a rather dangerous addiction. I do notice now that whenever anybody does anything which prevents me from having an ordinary morning writing, I'm in a sort of gloom. I feel as if I've been deprived of some necessary ingredient of the day.'

'If it is an addiction, why is it so dangerous?'

'Well, the reason it might be dangerous is that one would become like the Lady of Shalott, only capable of looking at the world through the mirror of art, and weaving it in one's magic tapestry. Whereas it could be said that life is real and life is earnest, and I should go out and find out what it's like – not write about it in books.'

He sees another danger too:

'There is always a danger of novelists, particularly novelists working in the realist tradition (as I do), of believing one's own tale a little bit too firmly, of thinking, "Because I've put it in a book, well, that's the way people are." Of course, the more one becomes obsessed by it, and the more one does it, the less time one has to be an observer, the more one becomes simply a maker.'

'But that might produce better novels . . .'

'Well, if you think of very good novelists – like Iris Murdoch or Dostoyevsky – a vast amount of these great masters' time was spent in writing fiction. Dickens is a case in point. It could be said, in the case of all three, "Ah, but they're only creating their own world, they're not writing a commentary on events." I think that shows you in a way what the best fiction can do. It isn't meant to be the news. They are not meant to be journalists.'

People are sometimes shocked or puzzled, when they hear appalling stories about the lives of artists. A. N. Wilson is not surprised that artists are sometimes monsters.

'I think there are all sorts of funny things going on inside most people. I think that we're mixtures of monsters and angels – all of us; and if people who hadn't done remarkable things with their lives (such as write great books, or be painters, or become great statesmen) were subjected to the kind of scrutiny to which biographers subject artists and statesmen, they too would seem monsters. If you read a biography say of the man-in-the-street, he would be just as full of appalling contradictions as, let us say, Tolstoy was. Perhaps they'd be less violent than in that particular case. But I rather doubt it.'

Wilson wrote once that, far from the nastiness of an artist, or a writer, detracting from their art, appalling inconsistency, vanity or hypocrisy was a necessary ingredient for most art to grow. He still thinks that is probably true.

'I think the best things in a human life can only come out of the whole of human life, which involves our dreadfulness, our awfulness, our sin, as well as our virtue.'

He was writing about Picasso, who painted sometimes very unpleasant things, from the depth of experience.

'There are women who've turned into voracious monsters, feeding on men, and there are scenes which are potentially loving scenes, nudes and so forth, turned into slaughterhouses and images of horror – not real slaughterhouses, but emotional slaughterhouses.'

That is the way, he says, a lot of people have experienced sex and love and life.

'I don't think it means Picasso was a monster to see it, even though, perhaps if he hadn't been quite such a monster, he would have been, as it were, more polite. I think great artists are never polite – they might have good manners socially, but they realise that if you see a truth, you've got to tell it.'

One of the things which increasingly interests Andrew Wilson is the extent to which it is possible to tell the truth in narrative.

'In other words, how much narrative, with its dreadful plausibilities, is a deceptive thing, and how much it's a vehicle for truth-telling.'

He says if you think of the great Russian novelists – either Tolstoy's historical fiction or Dostoyevsky's explorations of emotional and religious crises in people's lives – what you are reading is a wonderful, readable, plausible account of things; and that is what makes you carry on turning the pages, and what makes you believe it.

'But actual experience, as most people have it, is not framed into any sort of shape; and most people allow experience to drift by without trying to seize or shape it.'

'Do you feel that by imposing a pattern, sometimes the novelist is distorting the greater truth? Or revealing a greater truth?'

'I think that the great novelists are revealing truth by this strange process which is pure art. It is purely artificial, after all, isn't it? I think that all lesser artists, to a greater or lesser extent, distort – they are bound to.'

'You were once quoted as saying that you thought the only good books you had written were biographies. Do you still feel that?'

'No', he laughed loudly. 'I certainly don't think that and I cannot believe I said it, but if I did, I was talking nonsense.'

He has now written biographies of Milton, Sir Walter Scott, Hilaire Belloc, and most recently, a long scholarly book on Tolstoy. He learned to read Russian, as part of the research. What brought him back to Tolstoy?

'He's never gone away, and I think if you write novels, you inevitably keep on turning back to the people who really know how to do it, and re-reading them – not to copy them, so much as to somehow soak up a little bit of the way it is done.'

He is just as preoccupied with Tolstoy now as he was when he began the biography.

'I'd do it all differently now, of course, but I think he's one of the world's great geniuses, and I think the questions that he asks, not only about Russia, but about the nature of life – that is to say, whether the Sermon on the Mount and the Christian ethic is a sort of universal law which is incumbent on all of us to try to obey, or whether it's a sort of lunatic counsel of perfection which we can't obey – that's an endlessly haunting question.'

Another question he finds endlessly fascinating is whether or not it is a fantasy that we all know within ourselves what is the best way to live.

'That is the question that really lies at the heart of his last great novel, *Resurrection*, which I like more and more actually. I can see it's not a great novel like *War and Peace*, but its flawed greatness is almost more interesting to me, almost more wonderful.'

Sara Maitland, reviewing the biography of Tolstoy, said that A. N. Wilson seemed to regard Tolstoy as rather a nitwit. Did he think that was very unfair?

'I don't think I used the word "nitwit" of that great man. Of course, poor Tolstoy made himself seem very foolish, it's true, and the simplemindedness with which he set about trying to live out the Gospel was most extraordinary. He genuinely thought it was possible to dispossess yourself, which it just isn't, of course, in this world. If you are a family man, and you've got children to educate, and a wife who doesn't want to lead the same life that you want to lead – namely that of an itinerant pauper – you can't give up all wealth suddenly, at the stroke of a pen, as he wanted to do.'

And Tolstoy made another mistake:

'He did what all people are tempted to do, when they think they're religious sages (which I'm afraid to say, poor old Tolstoy thought he was), they get seduced into having disciples and little groups, and they very quickly start feeling the halo round their own heads, and then they are ridiculous – of course they are. But the fact that human beings are ridiculous doesn't in my mind diminish their greatness.'

'Did you, as you were writing it, feel superior to Tolstoy?'

'Absolutely not, no. Not even when he seems to be getting up to the most ludicrous thoughts and actions, I wasn't superior to him.'

Take, for instance, Tolstoy's idea that total celibacy was enjoined by the gospel (Wilson himself doesn't think it is):

'To write and publish an afterword to this effect, when your wife is pregnant for the thirteenth time or whatever it is, that is a ludicrous thing to do, isn't it? And then the whole farce of Countess Tolstoy rushing off to the Emperor and getting lifted the imperial ban on an allegedly obscene story, so that she could include it in the collected works, not because she admired it, but so she could get the royalty.'

Wilson says there was a sort of tragi-comedy going on all the time, in the later part of Tolstoy's life, and one is bound to find it appalling, but also comic.

'He's sitting in his study writing some great treatise about universal love and the necessity to regard every man, woman and child as your brother, and then stomping down the stairs, bumping into his wife, and saying, "You poison the very air we breathe". You're bound to find inconsistencies of that kind. I don't think that means that I'm superior to him. I know I'm not.'

'Was there a point, while writing the book, that you felt the Sermon on the Mount was so hopelessly unrealistic, so unliveable, you wished to put it aside?'

'Yes, I feel that all the time. I put the Sermon on the Mount on the side all the time, insofar as it enjoins us to live as if there were no tomorrow, to live as if money doesn't mean anything, to live as if there was nothing in life to cause you resentment, nothing in life to excite lust, etc. Of course, one puts it aside all the time, but it won't consent to be put aside – it keeps on coming back to haunt you. And the contradictions are not necessarily in the Sermon on the Mount, they are in oneself.'

But was Tolstoy's approach to it the right one?

'Not necessarily. For one thing, the point of the gospel, as opposed to the Torah, the law, is that life doesn't necessarily resolve itself into a rule book, and I think what Tolstoy was trying to do was to take the gospel and say, "This is the law by which I am going to live. No hitting back when somebody hits me on the cheek, and no taking oaths".'

Wilson agrees with Tolstoy and the Quakers that if you take Christianity seriously, you should not take oaths in a court of law. But he argues that if you take a broader view of the New Testament, the Beatitudes in the Sermon on the Mount ("Blessed are the peacemakers; blessed are they that mourn; blessed are they that hunger and thirst after righteousness," etc), are not perhaps as

St Matthew wished to depict them – the new Torah given on the new mountain by the new Moses.

'What they are, in fact, is a series of endlessly frightening, disturbing questions about us as human beings, at the deepest psychological level.'

He quoted Jesus's words: 'You have heard that it was said by them of old time, "Thou shalt not kill" . . . but I say to you, "Whoever is angry with his brother without a cause, shall be in danger of the judgment".'

'That isn't, as it appears to be on first sight, a new rule. It is an examination of you at your deepest level. The instinct, of course, is to brush examinations of that sort aside, because they are too disturbing. What it involves is shaking up your entire life every time you think about them, because anger is part and parcel of your existence; lust is part and parcel of your existence.'

He went on:

'It's no good saying every time you lust that you've committed adultery in your heart. That notches up about a thousand and fifty adulteries a year for most people. What you've got to do is to accept your imperfection, which poor old Tolstoy, like all Manichees, was unable to do – he went on struggling for perfection.'

Andrew Wilson thinks that the deeper wisdom lies in the writings of St Paul, who, he says, appears to be a total lunatic, when you first read the Epistle to the Romans.

'But in the middle of it, the seventh chapter, he recognises there's a sort of cosmic principle in the fact that we fail all the time – that the good we want to do never gets done, the evil that we don't want to do is what we do. That isn't an accident, it isn't a hiccup, it's something that lies at the depth of what we are as people.'

In his writing about religion, A. N. Wilson often concentrates on the struggle of the individual, rather than on the shared experience of the fellowship of Christians. Isn't the fellowship and the experience of being together in faith central to an understanding of Christianity?

There was a long pause, before he answered.

'I think there's a sense in which the Bible and indeed the Christian religion itself is really the story of the human individual confronting the unknown, the unseen – that there's a slight illusion if you think it can ever be done collectively.'

Another pause.

'I think that one's experience of God, if you want to use that phrase, is something which is always done alone, and it may be, as someone once said, that having made the journey alone, you will find that you arrive together, with lots of other people. That's presumably what's intended in the apocalypse at the end of the New Testament – that there's this great choir of strange individuals singing their hymn to the Lamb.'

He made them sound very strange. He freely confesses that the parts of the New Testament he finds most difficult to swallow are those bits such as the Acts of the Apostles, which suggest it can be done communally.

'When I hear a phrase, such as the phrase in our prayerbook, "the blessed company of all faithful people", I know that I am lacking in my understanding of what that phrase means. Because, very often, when I'm in the blessed company of all faithful people – without in any sense wishing to stand apart from them (and I think church membership is awfully important, and all those things) – I find the things they say that concern them, or the things that interest them, or the things which they believe, are not necessarily the things I believe or am interested in, and I'm rather disturbed by that sometimes.'

He added slowly: 'I don't necessarily wish to see in purely negative terms why it is, for instance, that I can follow a week's debate in the General Synod of the Church of England, and find they are debating things which are of no possible interest or relevance to the way I look at life – and they are the blessed company of all faithful people, I suppose.'

— • —

# SARA MAITLAND

— • —

Born 27 February 1950; married Donald Lee, 1972; one
daughter, one son. Education: public school, St Anne's College,
Oxford. Career: Freelance academic researcher, 1972–3;
freelance journalist, 1973–. **Novels**: *Daughter of Jerusalem*
(Somerset Maugham Award), 1978; *Virgin Territory*, 1984; (with
Michelene Wandor) *Arky Types*, 1987. **Biography**: *Vesta Tilley*,
(1986). **Short stories**: (contributor) *Introduction 5*, 1973;
(co-author) *Tales I Tell My Mother*, 1978; *Telling Tales*, (1983);
(with Aileen Latourette) *Weddings and Funerals* (1984);
(co-author) *More Tales I Tell My Mother*, 1988; *A Book of Spells*
(1987). **Theology**: (editor) *Walking on the Water* (1983); *A Map
of the New Country* (1983).

# DAUGHTER OF JERUSALEM

— • —

'I believe', said Sara Maitland, taking a drag at her cigarette, 'in a God who will take risks. I believe in a God who is wild, not tamed.'

She was sprawled in an armchair, in blue jeans, grey sweater and sneakers, in the attic of a rambling 16-roomed Gothic vicarage in East London. From the window of the neighbouring kitchen, now spotted with rain, a grey sky hung heavily over the architectural wastelands of east London. Across the road, rain had begun to collect on the flat roofs of the impersonal blocks of post-war flats. Someone had thought to plant a few trees. In the yard in front of the decaying house and neighbouring church, a gust of wind stirred bits of old rag and paper. A dog barked in the the distance. 'I love it here,' she had said.

We were sitting in her study. The vicarage has the air of a student's house. But in the attic study, with its bright green walls, peeling paint, black armchairs, and books and papers dotted comfortably around, a Macintosh Plus word-processor gleams in pride of place on the desk.

On the mantelpiece is a picture of the singer, actress, toast of the British music-hall, male impersonator and great 'gender-bender', Vesta Tilley. Sara Maitland published her biography in 1986.

She writes mostly about women.

She began writing in the early 1970s:

'I felt there was almost an idealisation of women going on within the early women's movement, which was very nice and proper. But I also thought it was quite dangerous, and not the whole truth. I was very worried about the image of women as simultaneously little white baa-lambs, the perfect innocents, and also heroic, brave and strong, and somehow there was no gap between the two. It was that imaginative gap that I suppose I was looking for.'

Her second novel, *Virgin Territory*, published in 1984, is about a nun, who is triggered into crisis by the rape of another member of her community in South America. She comes on study leave to England, where she meets a gay feminist, Karen. As their friendship grows, each challenges the other to throw off some of their old ways of thinking.

'I hope that is the most intimate book I will ever write. It's probably as near to autobiographical writing as I want to go. That sounds rather a weird thing to say as none of the characters resemble any of my actual life circumstances.'

Among the intellectual questions in the book are, What are the implications if God is no longer going to be only male? If God is no longer purely male, what is going to happen to all those patterns of behaviour traditionally laid on women – for instance, virginity or heterosexuality? And what is the point, in a way, given how dangerous Karen believes it is, in having a male god at all?

'That's really the nun's problem. She feels totally intimidated by: a), her father; b), her father in heaven, who, if I may put it frivolously, seem to form a posse to hunt her down and make her behave in appropriately nunnish ways.'

Towards the end of the novel, the nun is drawn towards an affair with Karen. Some Christians were shocked by the novel, but the author received some very unexpected letters:

'Maybe many nuns who read it were shocked in the privacy of their convents, and didn't let me know. But I got some very affirmative letters from women religious, who wrote saying they were really glad I had written it, that it meant a lot to them, that they found it very useful theologically.

'Maybe since writing that book, I've moved away from writing about quite such violent and dangerous themes. I think that book did resolve a lot for me, although actually it was very painful to write.'

One of the reasons the writing was so difficult, she says, was that surprises emerged:

'In it, there is a badly brain-damaged child with whom our

poor nun has a relationship, if you can call it that. The child has a voice which is in counterbalance to the voice of the father. It is a voice of chaos. While this other bossy voice in her head is telling her to behave right and be good and brush her hair, and, you know, be obedient, the voice of this child is luring her towards chaos. That was a complete surprise to me, and particularly the highly poetical voice that the child speaks in.'

She is now writing much less about violence and much more about the positive things women do for each other.

'Whether that's because the times are gloomy for the women's movement, and we need a little bit of uplift, I don't know. I do think of myself as quite a political writer, but I'm not entirely sure how politics and the imagination fit together yet. It's something that I continually re-explore.'

She coughed her smoker's cough and lit another cigarette.

A thin woman, with long straight hair framing her angular face, with big, round eyes, she has a direct look and a nervous, jerky way of talking. She was born in 1950, in a family of six children brought up in Scotland and London. The Sloane Ranger handbook lists both her primary school and public school among the top five. Her daughter is said to have described her progress as starting at the top and working her way down.

'Mildred was trying to explain about class to a German friend of ours, which is quite a hefty subject for a twelve-year-old, as I think she then was, to take on. What she said is: "Daddy started at the bottom and is working his way up; Mummy started at the top and is working her way down. And I would rather be like Daddy".'

'Is what she said true?'

'Yes, broadly. I had an immensely privileged childhood in every sense of the word. It was both privileged in the sense of comfortable, and indeed one would have to say rich. It was also privileged in the sense of having parents who were deeply concerned about their children and deeply committed to their education – in fact, unusually so, I should think, for their class background, especially for their girls.'

In 1968, when she was reading English at Oxford, she became a socialist. Why? A pause.

'Because I think that the sort of conservatism and privilege

117

with which I was brought up is actually philosophically and morally wrong.'

Psychologically, she says, she needed to assert her independence from her close-knit family. But a more important reason was that she started meeting the sort of people she had not met as a child.

'Even at Oxford, working-class children who were clearly bright and privileged were still clearly disadvantaged in ways that seemed to me, and still seem to me, to be profoundly unfair. I also moved towards the left through getting to know a number of Americans who were Vietnamese war-resisters of one sort or another . . . When I was given those things to question, I really felt that the sort of class system in Britain is simply wrong, not acceptable. That it is too expensive for a society, a waste.'

That feeling has deepened in her ever since.

'I know quite a lot of people who were quite far to the left then, who have drifted centrewards. Or the centre has moved so far to the right, that they are now righter than they were. But for me, that commitment to a culture of equality remains terribly, terribly important – although it is very confusing also.'

Her commitment to feminism emerged from a similar root. In January 1970, she went to hear Germaine Greer speak – it was before *The Female Eunuch* was published in Britain.

'She was pretty stunning actually . . .' She laughed. 'She would not like this, but she was a John-the-Baptist style prophet. She was much better at being a prophet in the wilderness than she was at relating to feminism as a communal movement. But anyway, she was magnificent, and I also met at that meeting somebody who became my close friend. I think perhaps, that if there hadn't been somebody to do it with, I wouldn't have found it so easy to do. I mean, friendship seems to me the core to the whole experience of feminism.'

Later that year, the first national women's liberation conference was held in Oxford. Spurred on by this, Sara Maitland joined the women's liberation movement.

'It was terrific fun, and suddenly all these people were popping up. At a more serious level, I think I became a feminist because I was very bright, I had very good friends, I had very interesting politics to think about, I had a basically loving family (although I was quarrelling with them quite a lot at this point), and I was extremely unhappy. And most of the women I knew were unhappy. And people increasingly called their unhappiness neurotic or insane. What feminism did was to explain it – "Of course you're unhappy, you're on to a really bad deal!" As soon as that's articulated, it fitted in with the framework of why I was a socialist. It's not fair, it's too expensive, it is wasteful of human talent, the discrimination of people because of class, because of race, because of gender. It is wasteful and unfair and wicked. That sounds very high-minded, but I think I really do believe it.'

An apparent irony in her life is that her husband, an American, is implacably opposed to any attempt to ordain women to the priesthood. He is a priest on the high-church Anglo-Catholic wing of the Church of England. On theological grounds, he believes a woman cannot be a priest. If the Church of England were to decide to proceed with their ordination, he is one of those priests whose consciences might lead them to leave the Church.

They married in June 1972, when he finished his finals. She was twenty-two, and he was just about to start training as a clergyman. She had become a Christian a few months before. Her husband still keeps and celebrates the exact date.

'I was reading a book in my bedsitter in West Paddington, where I was living at the time, and I had been thinking a lot about Christianity fairly newly, and talking about it a lot with my friends. Suddenly, it struck me I couldn't go on talking about it, that I had reached a point where I either had to say, "I believe this," or "No, I don't", and that if I did, then I had to do something about it. It was very, very clear to me, that it had moved from being an option, a philosophical idea, to being something very, very real. It was very early in the morning – and I got up and drove to Oxford to see my friends, in particular to see the person I am now married to. Just to tell them. It was then about 3.30 or 4 o'clock in the morning.

'I must say that apart from my husband, they were not at all glad to hear it. I got back in my car and I arrived back in London in time for work.'

She says that decision was irrevocable.

But there were immediate problems – like reconciling Christianity with feminism.

'It was very weird. What I did was simply to split the thing into two halves: I really didn't accept that for me the basis of Christianity is our one humanity in Jesus, and that therefore equality is not just a matter of civil rights or good law, it is a matter of primary and ethical obligation. I was a very old-fashioned high-church Anglo-Catholic spike; and a very progressive socialist feminist. It was difficult. None of the Christians that I then knew were remotely interested in feminism; and equally, none of the feminists I then knew were remotely interested in Christianity. They tended to think, "Ah, poor lamb", I think. The ones who liked me thought, "Poor dear. She'll grow out of it. It's a phase she's going through. What a pity really. A bit crazy." Or else, they were very hostile. A hostility which I can entirely understand.'

For some feminist friends, her getting married was almost as much of a problem as her becoming a Christian.

'There we were, sitting around diagnosing the whole state of marriage as being one of the primary forms of the oppression of women: so for anyone actually to go and do it was a very, very deep betrayal of a lot of people's hopes and visions. There were people who were already married before they became feminists, but that was a rather different thing. I was the first of our set, that I knew best then, to get married.'

'Do you think you began to write to resolve contradictions that you felt within yourself between Christianity and feminism?'

'I think that is interesting because I had in fact started writing about a year before I actually became a Christian. The first story I ever had published was a story about suffragettes; and oddly enough (it is very easy to psycho-analyse your own material after you have done it), it is about a woman who has just got involved in militancy, trying to make up her mind whether to marry a clergyman . . . At that time, I don't think I even knew Donald . . . What she tries to do is balance two ethics. What sort of anger is legitimate? Whether one is allowed to be angry? Whether you can be really angry, if you are going to marry and have the privileges of that as well? It is actually a rather good short story. I like it for other reasons as well – the first grown-up thing I ever wrote.'

Sara Maitland explored similar ideas in her first novel, *Daughters of Jerusalem*, which was published in 1978, and won the Somerset Maugham award for a first novel the following year. It is a step further on from the short story, because it is about a woman who has already made a choice. Elizabeth wants to get pregnant, but is unable to conceive. Her gynaecologist believes that a psychological barrier is preventing the pregnancy. But the novel is not just about barrenness. It's about friendships, choices, betrayals, conflicts and hopes. At the end of each of the nine chapters, each marking a month in the year, the author retells a Bible story about women. Each story is related to the contemporary story of Elizabeth.

'I suppose I think the job of great fiction (not that I'm suggesting *Daughters of Jerusalem* is great fiction) is to discover something about the whole by examining the minute. Even if you are reading a great novel about a third-century Eskimo, it should tell you as much about yourself as it tells you about third-century Eskimos.'

To help her do that, she has been quite blatant about dragging into her writing mythological themes or fairy or other stories:

'A story that has lasted five thousand years, as in the case of the Old Testament stories, has got to be a better story than I am going to make up in my study on a Tuesday afternoon. So I did want to draw parallels between that very legendary and all-so-long-ago experience of barrenness and of women's friendships – not to contrast them, but to underline how those experiences weren't a barmy new trend in feminism, but were fundamental to a whole kind of imaginative experience, and that those stories, right there at the roots of our history, somehow got buried.'

The story she likes best is the story of Deborah, the prophetess and Judge of Israel, who successfully led the Israelites against the Canaanite forces under Sisera. In the Book of Judges, chapter five, Deborah sings a song of triumph in which she recounts the victory and the murder of Sisera by a woman, Jael. The story is related to a point in the novel where the heroine is unfaithful to her husband under stressful circumstances:

'She goes to see her best friend, feeling terribly guilty, and the two of them work themselves up to a splendid fury against men, their general behaviour, the awfulness of her bloke, the awfulness of her friend's husband, the awfulness of the man she did in fact sleep with. And they get rid of the guilt by getting furious. And that is contrasted with the story of Deborah and Jael, when Jael puts the tent peg through Sisera's head, and Deborah creates for her this wonderful song of victory about how the stars in their course are fighting against Sisera. Her name will be great and remembered for ever. This extreme violent act against a man, who is technically the enemy, will live.

'There are things like that. The kind of anger of feminists is not just something to do with us uppity women right now; it is in the Bible right there in terms of victorious anger against a man. It is a most extraordinary song, and it is one of the oldest bits of the Bible that we now have.'

Another section of the Bible retold and reflected upon in the novel is St Luke's account of Mary's visit to her cousin Elizabeth, after the Angel Gabriel tells her she will bear a child, and her song of praise to God. It seems to Sara Maitland to be the triumph song of all Christianity:

'Luke is such a bloody good writer. He nearly always gets it emotionally spot on. That whole patterning of the annunciation and the visitation moves me deeply, deeply – I hope it is where we are all going: that we'll be able to say, "Because of what God has done for me, all generations will call me blessed." It is a very deep kind of pride in identity, in being beloved; and when everybody can sing that for themselves, then there is no question in my mind, that the mighty will be put down from their seats . . . Sorry, I'm getting into a little ecstasy here. But it just seems to me that is another story about women's friendship. It is rather nicer and more positive than Deborah and Jael.'

'You write about these women as if you just believe they are your close friends . . .'

'Oh yes, I have no doubt about that at all. I get quite laughed at, actually. When I wrote my theology book, the one about women in the church, there is an acknowledgement section, where I acknowledge the assistance I received from Teresa of Avila and the Blessed Virgin Mary.'

Many feminists have just given up on the church, walked out on it as irredeemably patriarchal and sexist, in language, structure and hierarchy. They have expressed their spirituality in other ways. Why has she not done that?

'It is not, for me, an option. For me, it is absolutely simple. I do believe in the incarnation; I do believe that at a historical and specific time, that which is eternal, unnamed, without qualities, all these things, broke through the barrier that exists between time and eternity. And that was Jesus; and that was, most inconveniently for all of us, male. And that, yes, God became human, that the word became flesh and blood and dwelt among us. And that that was a unique historical event.

'If you believe that, you cannot just jettison Christianity – you can't just say, "It's not good enough". It is just impossible. Sometimes, I wake up in the morning and think, "Wouldn't it be nice, wouldn't it be handy if that conviction, that faith just went away?" If I could say, "I don't believe a word of it – it's a nice interesting myth for our time". But I have never come to that point. I believe, in fact, more and more, as I get older.'

Sara Maitland has two children – a daughter who is sixteen and a son of eight. They, and the parish, help keep her grounded, when she is writing. One of her practical responsibilities in the parish is looking after the Shoreditch Council of Churches bus.

'The parish bus is my cross, and I must carry it. For five years, I have been trying to get the blinking bus off my back. It is just one of those things – everybody has them – like chronic dripping loos (we have another one), or shower. There is a gap between the shower and the bath, and no matter what, the water runs through.'

But she increasingly spends most of the school day working. Isn't the vicarage doorbell always ringing?

'The doorbell is always ringing, but I am not always answering it. I have just reached a new discipline which is to take the phone out at least for the morning session of work. I suppose I do find it difficult if someone rings up. I find a split in myself – whether to say, "Sorry, I'm busy", which is somehow true to myself, or not to. I feel I don't always get it right. But I certainly feel I have the right to and that right would be recognised.

'If people ring up and say they want a priest, then that is quite easy. The more difficult ones are people who don't know what they want. They desperately want to talk about something – say their mother is dying – and they feel the vicarage is the right place to ring. But it wouldn't occur to them that what they specifically want is a priest. They see the whole thing as a package – even if I said I was his secretary, they would still want to speak to me. But then, people don't ring about matters as urgent as that four times a day. Donald is here a lot, so I don't see that as a problem.'

In the book *Arky Types*, a collection of fictional letters, which she co-authored with Michelene Wandor, Sara Maitland mulled over some of the difficulties of writing. She seems to need to disillusion readers from the notion that books, like mountains, are just there.

'There are two things that people say to me socially that drive me up the wall. One is, "Are you writi..g anything at the moment?" To which, as a professional writer, the only thing to say to people who work in shops, is, "Are you selling any shoes at the moment?".'

'The other is – and this is even worse, "Oh, I always felt I could write a book if I had the time." Some people seem to think there is a great sort of book fairy in the sky, who has this range of people called authors, and just sits chucking books randomly, over the edge, and it lands in the author's lap, and it is published with their name on the front. However unautobiographical or fictional a book is, it still comes out by hard work, by blood, sweat and tears. It is not holy.

'It is worse for poets. Poetry is regarded as somehow so sort of mystical and holy. Though nobody ever reads any. People venerate poets. I just think it would be more useful to poets, if people read poetry.'

'Do you think that *Arky Types*, which explores some of these difficulties, was a bit self-congratulatory, a shade cosy?'

'Oh, yes, the book was amazingly self-congratulatory. I think that is one of its charms myself.'

'But isn't that one of the dangers of feminist writing – that it tends to narrow to a particular audience? And quite a narrow audience really . . .'

'Well, *Arky Types* has sold more copies, I think, than first copies of any other book I have ever written. So some people somewhere must like it. I like writing with another author very much. It is enormous fun. It is buoyant. I know people who don't think it is at all funny. But the person who typed it for us – who is not a literary person or a feminist – said she laughed so much, she had to turn the typewriter off. My jaw dropped.'

In *Arky Types*, one of the authors (it's not clear which) complains they will go 'stark, staring bonkers' if they have to read one more novel about the adulteries of the upper classes. The nineteenth-century social realist novel, they say, has been totally abandoned now for the petty realist novel. So, whose novels does Sara Maitland read and enjoy? She mentioned modern female novelists: Angela Carter, Emma Tennant, and a Canadian writer, Arethea van Herk, whose novel *No Fixed Address* was published in 1988 by Virago.

'It is an incredibly good novel. It does what I am most interested in doing, which is walking either side of that line between
fantasy and reality – very pinned down, very specific concrete
details, that are perfectly real, and at the same time, completely
bouncing off the walls with imaginative energy.'

She thinks many twentieth-century novels, of the petty social
realist category, are trapped within their own self-importance, and
lack the intellectual stature of which nineteenth-century novelists
were so unafraid.

'I think there is a paucity of intellectual ideas about anything
except writing. An awful lot of novels are about the structure of the
novel, the writing of the novel, about the sex life of the novel writer
and his or her three friends. A great deal of very good non-fiction is
being written at the moment about the effects of Thatcherism in
this country; but I do not know a fiction novel in Britain that even
attempts to address that, not at a serious level.'

'Do you think the church is in as bad a way as the great novel?'

'Yes, I do. . . . Someone once described organised religion as
ethics tinged with sentiment, and I think an awful lot of churches
are content to be that, rather than to be the ordered channel of
revelation. For one thing, I think one of the tests of the
effectiveness of churches is the capacity to prophesy. And I don't
see an awful lot of prophetic vision.'

Again and again, her conversation returns to images, dreams,
ideas from the Bible. But sometimes she will retell Bible stories
from different perspectives. In her short story, *Triptych*, she
considers the Biblical account of how the patriarch Abraham
banishes to the desert the slave girl Hagar, and her son by
Abraham, Ishmael. This is after Abraham's formerly barren wife,
Sarah, has a child. She tells the story first from Hagar's point of
view, then from Sarah's. She then, as a polemical joke, refuses
point blank to give Abraham's perspective. She says Father
Abraham lives off his wife's immoral earnings, and describes him
as 'frankly a real bastard, almost certainly insane, demonstrably
selfish, autocratic, lecherous, cowardly, violent and a megalo-
maniac to boot.'

She reckons that everybody in the West knows something
about Abraham, so no story teller could destroy that story by
playing with it.

'The better known a story, the more liberties you can take with it . . . Abraham does live off his wife's immoral earnings. It says so in Genesis. But all these fundamentalists telling us how we ought, or ought not to be behaving, and what sort of sex or sexuality we ought to have, base it on the Bible. Either Abraham, in their terms, is frankly a right bastard, or living off your wife's immoral earnings is OK.'

She feels equally strongly about Abraham offering his son Isaac as a sacrifice to God:

'Either you are talking about an entirely weird God, or somebody who sees his son as something that is available for sale to God for some higher option. I just think that story is bizarre and yet, we in the Christian West are heirs of Abraham. And proud of it. We should jolly well look at our past with some clarity.'

'But many Christians would say that that story is about trust, about trusting God, about acceptance that everything you have comes from God. It is a symbol of offering it back to God, and it foreshadows the offering of God of his own son, Christ . . .'

'A bloody dubious moral act of substitution . . . If one is going to take that path, I must assume that Christ offers himself in the will of the father, not that the father somehow offers the passive son . . . I suppose of course, the moral of the story is that you can trust God for anything and everything. But that story must have read damned oddly to Jews in Auschwitz.'

Sara Maitland once described herself as a terrible moralist at heart. She has no wish now to disown that.

'As a writer, yes, I think I am. I really do care about morals. I think that writing that does not care about moral conduct, or fiction writing that is not about moral conduct, is not about anything, in a way. I laugh when I say that because I think, in Christian terms, a great number of people regard me as totally immoral . . . or an amoral libertarian.'

She believes that writers have to take some responsibility for the characters they invent, and what the characters do; that writers have to stand constantly in judgment over themselves and their own text.

'I do think writing is terribly important. But I don't think it is as important as living well, as treating other people well, growing oneself. Living well is the most important thing in the world.'

'Do you see God now as a female God?'

'No. I certainly don't see Jesus, even in some super resurrected state, as female. I don't think I see the first person of the Trinity, or that which is traditionally called God the Father, as either male or female. I would be very careful grammatically never to construct God as only male, in writing or speaking, because I think that is logical and also theologically correct . . . I don't see the Holy Spirit as male or female either.'

'What sort of God do you believe in?'

She paused for a long time, her head thrown back, her eyes shut tight.

'A God who is wild, not tamed . . . I have tried to read recently some new physics. A god who can work out "quarks inside atoms" does not need gender, and rule books and stuff.'

The pace of her voice quickened.

'I feel we are all trying to pin God down and make him manageable: "You must say 'he', and you mustn't say 'she'; you must define the trinity in this particular way. You must have dogmas for this, that and the other." . . . There's a wonderful, wonderful book by a woman called Annie Dillard, called *Pilgrim at Tinker's Creek*. At one point, she says, "If I were God, and had dreamed up the brilliant idea of creating something, I'd have made do with a tiny little glob of matter." That, in itself would have been such a brilliant notion. Instead, what do we get? A kind of God who seems perfectly happy to have three million five hundred different forms of insect life.

'The whole thing is so *abandoned* . . .' she said, making a big sweep with her arms. 'I believe in this enormously generous God, so enormous that the whole universe can be contained within the Godness of God . . . I am awestruck by God . . . That's the sort of God I believe in.'

— • —

# BRIAN MOORE

— • —

Born, 25 August 1921; married Jean Denney. Guggenheim fellowship, (USA), 1959; Canada Council Senior Fellowship (Canada), 1960; Scottish Arts Council International Fellowship, 1983. **Novels**: *The Lonely Passion of Judith Hearne*, 1955 (film, 1989); *The Feast of Lupercal*, 1956; *The Luck of Ginger Coffey*, 1960; *An Answer from Limbo*, 1962; *The Emperor of Ice-Cream*, 1965; *I am Mary Dunne*, 1968; *Fergus*, 1970; *The Revolution Script*, 1972; *Catholics*, 1972 (W.H. Smith Literary Award, 1973); *The Great Victorian Collection*, 1975 (James Tait Black Memorial Award, 1976; Governor-General of Canada's Fiction Award, 1976); *The Doctor's Wife*, 1976; *The Mangan Inheritance*, 1979; *The Temptation of Eileen Hughes*, 1981; *Cold Heaven*, 1983; *Black Robe*, 1985 (Heinemann Award, RSL, 1986). **Non-fiction**: *Canada* (with Editors of Life), 1964.

# CATHOLICS

— • —

'I would like to believe in something', said Brian Moore. 'And I am interested in people that do believe in something. But I don't know what to believe in. I think writing novels is for me a way of protection against the meaninglessness of life, which I think about a lot.'

He was sitting behind an ancient green-baize-covered table in a studio in the basement at Broadcasting House. A train on the Bakerloo line rumbled past in some neighbouring subterranean cavern. It was five-and-a-half thousand miles away from the sparkling Pacific breakers on the stretch of sunlit sand in Malibu where his home now is. But not as far away as the grey Belfast of his childhood in the 1920s and early 1930s at the tail end of the Great Depression, with its poverty and unemployment, its religion and class hatred. His first thought as a young man when he had a chance was to leave Northern Ireland.

'Do you hate Ireland?'

'No, I don't hate Ireland. But I didn't like my school. I was not religious as a child.'

Brian Moore has the distinction of being one of the few boys from his Roman Catholic secondary school who never had a vocation to be a priest.

'I used to say it was a priests' factory. It was quite a hard school, it still exists. We were beaten all the time. We were caned if we failed to recite our French irregular verbs properly in the morning. You were caned for every mistake you made. So that you go through the entire day being beaten on the hands, day in, day out, everything was taught by rote. It was really a totally inferior method of teaching people, and I am still very angry when I think about it. This was a Catholic school in a predominantly Protestant milieu; therefore we had to get better marks than the Protestant schools. We were then beaten and coerced into achievement, and we weren't really taught anything. I remember when I first went to France, no one could understand the French I was speaking, not one word of it. Yet I knew all my irregular verbs.'

'What about the religious side?'

'I think some people are just naturally not religious. My memory of it always is of telling lies in confession. I couldn't honestly confess my sins to a priest, and therefore I was in a state of 'sin' when I made my first communion. And because of that, I began to question the whole of religion at an early age.'

He ran his thin fingers across his forehead.

'I started fudging it in confession and I was told this was a mortal sin, and after a while, I think out of pure self-protectiveness, I, like most children in my situation, said, "After all, this is a lot of nonsense, it's got to be a lot of nonsense. No one's going to kill me. I'm not going to die." But I was still influenced by it until I was about 18 or 19. And then I had a chance to go overseas with the British Ministry of War Transport. I went to North Africa, and, as the Irish would say, I never darkened a church door again.'

'You've literally never been to a church since?'

'Well, I'll go in to look at them, I'm quite fascinated by them, but I've never prayed or ever had any religious inclination since. This surprises people, because I write a lot about Catholicism.'

Indeed he does.

He had arrived at Broadcasting House ten minutes early, looking neat and sprightly, a courteous, slightly Puckish figure of 67 going on 48. He talks in a quick-witted, lively Irish fashion, full of stories. He still pronounces his name the Gaelic way: Breean.

In 1987, Brian Moore published a thriller about political and religious compromise. Called *The Colour of Blood*, it was nominated for the Booker Prize and won the Sunday Express Book of the Year award. The main character is a cardinal in a country in Eastern Europe, possibly Poland, who believes that, despite intense pressure, it is better to go on day by day improving things than to resort to violence. Moore says the book emerged not so much from his experience of Ireland as a young man, but out of his reading about what happened in the 1960s after he had left it as an exile. The other influence was Poland. After the war, he had worked in Eastern Europe for the United Nations Relief and Rehabilitation Administration. At one stage, he interviewed Cardinal Wyszinski, who made a compromise with the communists. The cardinal was arrested, and spent two years incarcerated, and then came out and made a concordat with the state.

'It made me realise how much I hate terrorism, how much I hate the present violence, and how much I feel that the IRA and terrorists in various other places have swept to centre stage so that no one pays any attention to moderate people who might be trying to solve these things in a peaceful way.'

He invented a fictional country, because he didn't want to be tied to events by history.

'It is very difficult to write about any real country now, because next week's headlines may make you out-of-date. So I used a country that wasn't Poland, but had a lot of Poland's problems, and at the same time, subliminally in my mind, I must have thought of Northern Ireland, because in the book I have police stopping you, and soldiers searching cars – the kind of things that happen in Northern Ireland and do happen also in Eastern European countries.'

He chose the figure of the cardinal because he wanted to write about a good man.

'The aim of the Catholic church is to save people's souls. And to do that, they must keep the churches open. They must make a *modus vivendi* with Caesar; they must try to get the schools going; and if they take a totally negative view in a communist country with a communist government, they will be shut down. That's what Cardinal Glemp and what these people realised. The Pope was, I think, rather irresponsible coming along and talking about Solidarity, which everyone knows cannot win in a no-win situation.'

'That's a pretty strong word, "irresponsible" . . .'

'Well, he was irresponsible, because he gave them the hope that if they spoke up against the government a bit more, maybe there would be some support. But the Vatican has never supported Poland. Eastern European Catholics, and Eastern European people generally do not trust the West. I live in America. Americans think if they just went in tomorrow to Poland or to Russia, everyone would rise up in the streets and say, "My god, isn't this wonderful. Here comes democracy!" They have no idea that this is totally untrue. These people do not want to become Americans.'

When *The Colour of Blood* was given the Sunday Express prize, one of the judges, the journalist and writer, Auberon Waugh, disassociated himself from the award, because he said the book advocated conciliation with the communists. The author responds that Mr Waugh didn't know what he was talking about.

'I was quite delighted he would think that about me, because he is a person whose politics are not mine, and I do believe in conciliation for the Church. I also believe it is very dangerous for the Church to back anything remotely like terrorism. It is against the Christian religion, number one, and secondly, when I see these priests at IRA funerals, I feel there is something absolutely wrong with some of the speeches they make. For that reason, I do believe in moderation, and I think that's what Waugh didn't understand – that I was talking about being civilised and not uncivilised.'

All Brian Moore's family were Catholics except for his grand-father, a solicitor, who was originally a Protestant.

'He changed his religion when he was very young, for reasons I can't understand, because he must have lost most of his practice when he did that.'

He died when Brian Moore's father was twelve, so his father, the chief surgeon at Belfast's largest Catholic hospital, had to put himself through school and university by winning scholarships.

'I don't think he was super-intelligent, but he was a wonderful exam-passer.'

Brian Moore himself was 'dismal' at maths, 'and if you failed to get a pass mark in maths, you failed the whole exam. My father was very gentle with me, but he was disappointed in me, because I didn't go on, like my brothers, to be doctors and get easily into university and that sort of thing.'

The author's mother came from the Republic, from Donegal, and he would go on holiday to his mother's people there. It was a totally different world from the city.

'They were not as well off as my father. I was a child on a farm so I saw the rural side of Irish life, which was wonderful. And then I would also be sent to Dublin, which, if you can believe it, seemed like Paris to me. I stayed with my cousin who had a big house on Phoenix Park. These were holiday places. I live on the sea now, I think, because every summer, my father always took a house for a month at some Irish seaside place.'

Irish nationalist politics featured strongly in his childhood. His uncle – a very nice man, he says, like his father, and a university professor – was the head of the non-political forerunner of the IRA. He went down in history as countermanding the Irish rising on Easter Sunday:

'He told them to go home. That wasn't a popular move, but he was quite right. The rising was a failure. People tend to forget that.'

By the time Brian Moore was a young man, he was sick of Irish politics. 'I was sick of these old battles, which seemed to me to be over a very long time ago, and to be very parochial. I felt they hadn't created a free Ireland, they had created what I called a Grocers' Republic of very small-minded people.'

What drew him instead was the creative energy bursting out of writers like W. H. Auden and T. S. Eliot, and the left-wing politics of the era. By then he was secretly nursing a hope to become a writer, because he had always won essay prizes and so on at school.

'Then I read James Joyce, and of course the whole romantic Joycian notion of art as a religion (which now seems terribly old-fashioned) did influence me, because it all tied in. I could go for the religion of art, and drop real religion. And I could go for international politics, world revolution and drop the poor old Irish revolution that we're sick of. It was very attractive to me at that time.'

He smiled across the green baize, a slightly sad smile.

For someone whose own Catholic experience was so negative, Brian Moore seems a novelist obsessed with Catholic themes and ideas, however varied and unexpected the setting. He says, not entirely convincingly, that he uses religion as a metaphor for any sort of belief, and that writing about religion just happens to be easier than writing about belief, say, in world revolution. A more convincing answer is that it enables him to write about crisis. He discovered this in his first novel, *The Lonely Passion of Judith Hearne*, which has now been released as a film with the actress Maggie Smith in the title role.

'I said to myself, "I'd like to write abut someone losing his faith," and then, of course, there loomed up the horrible shadow of James Joyce and *Portrait of the Artist as a Young Man*. I said, "I can't compete with that". And then I said, "What if it were some lady like the spinster lady, who used to come to our house to see my mother on Sunday afternoons? What if one of those people were waiting for something great to happen in her life, and it didn't happen?" And, through innocence really, I decided to write it from a woman's point of view, not knowing what a danger that was for a male novelist. And I had great luck, because it was successful and women liked it and felt that it was sympathetic to them, and the book had an extraordinary life. It never was a bestseller, but it's never been out of print in thirty years.'

'Though, originally, it was turned down by ten American publishers?'

'Twelve, I think. They felt it was too depressing, and the woman was not attractive, and she was religious. She was silly, genteel, and she was a very difficult character to make a heroine of; but people did identify with her plight.'

That choice of a central character facing crisis is a trademark of many of Brian Moore's novels. He seems absorbed by failure, rather than success. When he begins a novel, he does not know what will happen, but he does know that whatever it is his characters want, whatever it is they believe, whatever illusions they have, are just now about to be taken away from them, and they will be forced to re-examine their lives within something like the Greek unities, within a certain framework of time; and at the end of it all, he hopes there will be some catharsis and something will change. When Judith Hearne discovers she doesn't believe in religion any more, she also discovers she cannot tell anyone this, so she has to hide her lack of faith and pretend to go to Mass. All the things which used to be the only joy in her life are now a mockery. But the very end is left open. We do not know what her future will be.

'If the book is open-ended in that way, readers quite like it. They don't think they are going to like it, but they wonder what will happen to her. "Would she go mad?" People ask themselves that question afterwards. I love that. If I can create the illusion that the character is really a living person, then the novel is a success.'

Critics have often spoken in glowing terms of Brian Moore's

understanding of the psychology of women. I wondered whether the fact that he had a very close relationship with his mother and sisters made him more interested in women than men?

'Yes, I think the fact that I had six sisters and that I was one of my mother's favourite sons, if not her favourite son, had an effect on me, because I was listening to women talk and to girls talk a lot, because I didn't go to boarding school.'

'Why do you find women so interesting?'

'In a curious way they are more honest when they talk to you. Women live in a personal world, a very, very personal world. Men, I find, are always, as they say in America, "rolling their credits" at each other. They come on telling you what they've done, and who they are, and all the rest of it. Quite often, women don't do that, because life hasn't worked out that way for some of them. But when a woman tells me a story about something that happens to her, you often get a sudden flash of frankness which is really novelistic. It is as if a woman knows when she tells a story that it must be personal, that it must be interesting. Men often see the story as something about them, rather than the true story.'

I was still curious as to how he gets into women's thoughts and emotions so well. One answer is that he falls in love with his characters.

'I was reading something fascinating recently about Tolstoy. When he started writing *Anna Karenina*, he hated her. He thought she was a cheap sort of woman, an adulteress. But in the course of the book (he had a fantastic eye for how people really looked and behaved), he fell in love with her. She changed then, in his mind. She became a more attractive character. But fifteen years later, when he was asked about the book, he said it was a cheap story about adultery. He had had his love affair with the character and ended it. When I read that, I thought no matter what you think about Tolstoy – he was absolutely terrible about women, he was a monster, the macho king of all time – for the period in which he wrote the novel he *became* the character. And that, I feel, is the true thing in novel-writing.'

When Brian Moore is writing a novel, he becomes quite obsessed with the characters. He reckons that a lot of the writing is done in sleep at the end of the day.

'You don't know you're dreaming about them, but when you wake up the next morning, suddenly you are able to go on, you make the next move. But when the novel's over, and someone says to me, "What about Sheila Redden (in *The Doctor's Wife*)?", I feel, "Who?", because it's like an old love affair that I don't feel any more. I don't think about the characters after the novel is written. I love seeing the book come in, printed, bound and finished, but from that moment on, it's hideous, because you have to face reviewers, you have to face publicity, it's not your book any more.'

'But you do fall in love with women when you are writing about them?'

'Yes, but not only with the women. I fall in love with the male characters too. Not so much fall in love with them, but try to become them. Try to understand them. I never like Dickens, because Dickens uses caricature characters. I don't like flat characters. Even if I've got a very small character who maybe only makes an appearance for one scene, I try to think, "Wait a minute now, he must have two sides to him."'

Brian Moore came to be living in California by accident. 'Every place I've lived in my life has been totally accidental.' He went to North America first in pursuit of a Canadian girl who was older than he was. In Montreal, she said she wasn't interested in him and he was left there, stranded. He worked for a while as a construction clerk, then as a journalist. He wound up in New York because, after his first two novels, he won a Guggenheim scholarship which dictated that in order to pick up the money, he had to live in the States.

He originally moved to California to do a screenplay for *Torn Curtain* for Hitchcock, because he was broke. His Canadian wife loved the climate, and they stayed. They live on a beach, but he says it's not the Malibu that people think of as movie-star land. The nearest shop is four miles away, and it's quite remote. He discovered that he had no social life there, and that that was wonderful for writing novels. He had peace and quiet. So he lives there eight months every year. He teaches for part of that time, because, he says, 'it's a way to meet twenty-year-olds', and he's curious about what they really read – not much Scott Fitzgerald, he discovers, nor Saul Bellow, but quite a lot of Hemingway. Every year, he comes back to Europe. He likes to keep a foot in both places because he balances the two worlds one against the other in his mind.

Many of his novels have been set in places he has just left.

'When I started writing a book set in New York called *An Answer from Limbo*, I became terrified, because when I walked out every day, I would think, "I am setting this in Madison Avenue and Madison Avenue is changing in front of my eyes", and it was an uneasy feeling. There was no tranquillity, so I got a fellowship to come to London that year (I rented a house in Wellington Square in Chelsea), and that was where I wrote my New York book. I discovered then that it's right for me, to be away from the place I'm writing about. You see it as an exile or an outsider, and of course, that's been very much my life, writing about places after I've left them.'

*An Answer from Limbo* tells the story of a writer giving up everything for literary success. He says it was not semi-autobiographical:

'It was based on something I saw in New York, what tremendous literary jealousy people had, and the tremendous hunger for success that writers had. And they couldn't accept the fact that success might be gradual or partial, they wanted it all, everything at once. This was happening to a writer I knew, and it occurred to me, "What if I transmogrified him? Put myself into him and brought my mother over from Ireland? What would happen then?" You know, that's how novels get started.'

'You once said that writers need a core of dullness in their lives to write a novel . . .'

'I think so, because I don't like literary society. I wouldn't like to be going out to dinner and meeting the best minds of my generation all the time, because when you're writing a novel, you don't need to meet the best minds of your generation. You may be stuck with some boring character like Miss Hearne, or trying to put yourself into the mind of a cardinal, which is not something you can do after an evening's dinner party. So I need a lot of quiet to write novels.'

He says some people write two novels, maybe three, and then go off and do something else because they can't stand the loneliness of it. Other people, like him, are addicted to it.

'A lot of writers say writing is misery. You've heard all that. I don't believe that at all. I am not happy when I'm not writing, and I'm quite happy when I am writing, even if it's not going well. I know it's spurious, because it's not true, but it seems to give a purpose in my life which isn't there otherwise.'

Writing, he once said, is rather a selfish occupation. I reminded him of that.

'It is', he said simply. 'I mean, who do I write for? What difference will my novels ever make in the world? They won't make any real difference.'

He admires people who change things, who do things, who give themselves up to other people. He admires the idea of selflessness – 'which of course, is very Christian,' he says, with a wry laugh. He admires Mother Teresa:

'She may be a cunning old peasant, but she is also a person who could do things I could never do, like go down to the slums of Calcutta, and change people's lives . . . In other words, I believe in people who have beliefs. I don't have beliefs myself.'

I recalled that Winston Churchill said he was in relation to the Church rather like a flying buttress. He supported it from the outside. Was that true of him too? He laughed.

'I don't know. At this age, it might be. I was very hostile to it, I was very anti-clerical when I was young; but I don't think of the Church as one of my main preoccupations. I am interested in goodness, and it's a fact that saintly people are often connected with religions'.

Of all modern English-language novelists, Brian Moore is one of the most unexpected. Graham Greene said that Moore treats novels like a tamer treats a wild beast. Pick up the books of some novelists, and you can immediately guess the author. Moore's work is much less easily caught. He puts this down to the fact that after choosing exile from Ireland, he wrote out his own life in his first three novels, and then went to new places, had new experiences.

'Most days when you're writing a novel, it's slightly depressing. You say, "Here I am, a man sitting in a room, grown up, writing tales", and it doesn't seem a sensible occupation. And then, if it's not going well, you think, "Am I going to go on doing this for the rest of my life?" So one of the panaceas against that was to say, "Yes, but this time, I am trying something technically new". So I have written a number of books in a number of styles.'

For instance, *The Great Victorian Collection* is a fantasy, set very realistically, but a fantasy. *The Mangan Inheritance* starts as a novel of manners set in Canada, and then becomes almost a

Gothic novel. *The Colour of Blood* is a political and metaphysical thriller. *Fergus* touches on the surreal. Then there is *Black Robe*, about Jesuits and Indians in seventeenth-century Canada, one of his favourite books.

'I always hated historical novels. *Black Robe* is an historical novel, in a way, but it doesn't give you the heavy padding that historical novels do. They do a lot of research and then they must put the research in. I don't believe in that. Do a minimum of research, and then keep it out. Don't let it impede the story.'

The novel tells the story of one of the seventeenth-century Jesuits who went to Canada to convert the Indians.

'They were the only people who tried to learn the Indian languages, which were very difficult. They were mostly upper-class intellectuals and they were plunged into a country of terrible cold, filthy conditions, horrible food, really horrible food. The Indians were polygamous, they were cannibals, they had a strong and mystic religion of their own. It was at the very dawn of the North American experience when the Indian considered the white man as his inferior, and rightly so, from his point of view, because he couldn't hunt, he couldn't survive.

'To try to convert those people to Christianity was an incredibly difficult job, and a job in which they did not succeed.'

He based the novel on a story which was told about Father Noel Chabanel, one of the early Jesuits.

'One day, in the wilds of Canada, he said, "Oh, my God, I've got a degree in philosophy, what am I doing in this terrible place?" And at that point he said, "The devil has tempted me into these thoughts." So he knelt down and made a vow that he would spend the rest of his life with these terrible people in this terrible country. It was that sort of dedication I was interested in. In the course of writing the book, I realised that all of his beliefs would be challenged strongly in Canada, and if he was intelligent, he would have to wonder whether he was right, whether he ever would convert these people to his point of view, whether in fact he wouldn't be destroying their life by changing their behaviour. That's a perfect situation of crisis.'

Brian Moore regards the beginnings and endings of books as vitally important:

'If you read twenty or thirty pages by a writer, and want to continue, you are in his sea and swimming in that sea. He can write quite badly after that. Because by that time, you're in his sea, and you're moving forward . . . People say that I write quite simply, but they don't realise how much I rewrite. I rewrite a lot. I would rewrite the opening two or three pages maybe forty, fifty times until I had that sense that it was right. Then it's easy for me, because I set the tone by doing that.'

But at that point, he still has no idea what will happen at the end.

'It's like meeting someone at a party, and you come away and say, "What do we think of him?" You have an opinion about this person. But if you live with them for a month or two, you change your opinion of them completely. You develop, I hope, a sense of truth about them. You say, "Wait a minute, he couldn't, he wouldn't do that." So that approach, not knowing what is going to happen, saves you from what I find to be a weakness in many novels – the novelist solves his or her problems by sudden death, by extreme action, by something about which we say, "Hold on a minute, that doesn't seem quite right."

'Funnily enough, Hitchcock, when I worked with him, came up with a very similar idea. He was a fanatic about timetables. You know, "Does this airline fly here?" And then he would have his assistant run out and find that out. And I would think, "Who cares whether the Czech Airline flies into Poland on Wednesdays?" But he worried about all these things, because he said people have a curious sense of reality, which you cannot deceive. He said (he called it the ice-box idea), "When they come home from a movie, they reach in the ice-box and take out something to eat", and he said they say, "I don't think the train runs on Sunday from Charing Cross station. I don't think there are any trains on Sundays." "That's right, and did you notice something else . . ." and in twenty minutes your movie is destroyed, completely finished. So I've remembered the ice-box theory. You must be very careful to make it believable.'

In the 1960s, shortly after the end of the Second Vatican Council which introduced so many reforms into the life of the Catholic Church, Moore published a sombre novella called *Catholics*. It portrays a battle-dressed young American visiting a remote Irish monastery and putting an end to some of the old traditions of the Church. I wondered whether he was unduly fearful, at that time, of the changes that were happening?

'I didn't feel that at all. I had just had an amazing experience. I was in Nova Scotia with my wife, and we passed this church on Sunday morning, and I heard all this banjo music coming out, and I said, "What are they, Baptists?", and she said, "No, they're Catholics." I said, "They can't be Catholics." I hadn't been in the church for years. I went inside and I saw all these people playing and singing with guitars, and I couldn't believe it. This was supposed to be a Mass.

'Three weeks later, I was in a place called Clare Island in Ireland, which is very remote, on the west coast, and I saw one of these small old churches, and people trudging up to it the way they always have in Ireland, and I thought, "What if . . .?" And that is what happened.

Brian Moore says he doesn't have heroes or villains, that he took both sides of the argument and presented them. To him the book was not so much about changes in the Church, as about a man who had lost his faith:

'He simply goes on being abbot of the community, because he is the leader of the community, and he feels that his men need him, and the community needs him. He is absolutely miserable, and in deep depression, because he has no faith. He is a secular saint, in a sense, because he does it for the sake of others.'

At the end of the book, the abbot tells the other people (they are talking about miracles and the miracle of the Mass and so on), that there is only one miracle and that is prayer. He says that, if we pray, God comes.

'And he kneels down and tries to pray. God does descend on all the others and comforts them, but the abbot cannot pray. He doesn't have that gift. Graham Greene said once that faith is a gift, and I thought that was a very true remark. It's a gift I don't have.'

'You've given the impression that you dismissed religion very early on, and it really hasn't been for you at all. But nevertheless, I come back to this point that your novels seem to be really obsessed by religion and religious themes. Why is that?'

'I don't know. It would be easy to say that I would like to believe in something, and I think that in a sense that's true . . . Somehow or other, when I am writing, when I am inventing my own little world, I'm not thinking about what's happening to me. I look at someone like Joyce Carol Oates – she writes an incredible number of novels. I had an image of her, just sitting in a room, day in, day out, living a surrogate life.'

'So is novel-writing a way of escape, is that what you mean?'

'In some sense, it is, I think. It's a way of escape. It's a way of not thinking about what I haven't done with my life.'

— • —